An
Essex Christmas

An
Essex Christmas

Compiled by Humphrey Phelps

ALAN SUTTON

First published in the United Kingdom in 1993
Alan Sutton Publishing Limited · Phoenix Mill · Far Thrupp
Stroud · Gloucestershire

First published in the United States of America in 1993
Alan Sutton Publishing Inc · 83 Washington Street
Dover · NH 03820

British Library Cataloguing in Publication Data

Essex Christmas
I. Phelps, Humphrey
394.2663094267

ISBN 0-7509-0123-3

Library of Congress Cataloging in Publication Data
applied for

Cover picture: The Skater *by Edward John Gregory, reproduced by
courtesy of Richard Hagen Fine Paintings*

Typeset in 12/13 Garamond.
Typesetting and origination by
Alan Sutton Publishing Limited.
Printed in Great Britain by
WBC, Bridgend, Mid Glam.

Contents

Essex

JOHN NORDEN

John Norden, a map maker, wrote this in 1594.

This shire is most fatt, fruteful, and full of profitable thinges, exceeding (as far as I can finde) anie other shire, for the generall comodeties and the plentie. Thowgh Suffolke be more highlie comended of some wherwith I am not yet acquaynted But this shire seemeth to me to deserve the title of the Englishe Goshen, the fattest of the Lande, comparable to Palestina, that flowed with milke and hunnye. But I can not comende the healthfulness of it. And especiallie nere the sea coastes, Rochford, Denge, Tendering hundredes, and other lowe places about the creekes, which gave me a moste cruell quarterne fever. But the manie and sweete comodeties countervayle the danger.

Novelist in the Hunting Field

ANTHONY TROLLOPE

From 1859 to 1871 Anthony Trollope was living at Waltham
House. As well as writing some of his best novels at Waltham
Abbey he also, during the winter, hunted twice a week from the
kennels at Harlow.

Essex was the chief scene of my sport, and gradually I became known there almost as well as though I had been an Essex squire, to the manner born. Few have investigated more closely than I have done the depth, and breadth, and water-holding capacities of an Essex ditch. It will, I think, be accorded to me by Essex men generally that I have ridden hard. The cause of my delight in the amusement I have never been able to analyse to my own satisfaction. In the first place, even now, I know very little about hunting – though I know very much of the accessories of the field. I am too blind to see hounds turning, and cannot therefore tell whether the fox has gone this way or that. Indeed all the notice I take of hounds is not to ride over them. My eyes are so constituted that I can never see the nature of a fence. I either follow someone, or ride at it with the full conviction that I may be going into a horsepond or a gravel-pit. I have jumped into both one and the other. I am very heavy and have never ridden expensive horses. I am also now too old for such work, being so stiff that I cannot get on to my horse without the aid of a block or a bank. But I ride still after the

same fashion, with a boy's energy, determined to get ahead if it may possibly be done, hating the roads, despising young men who ride them, and with a feeling that life cannot, with all her riches, have given me anything better than when I have gone through a long run to the finish, keeping a place, not of glory, but of credit, among my juniors.

Calendar

HUMPHREY PHELPS

On 1 December the town crier of Colchester used to announce:

> Cold December has set in,
> Poor people's backs are clothed thin,
> The trees are bare,
> The birds are mutes;
> A pint of purl would very well suit.

On 6 December, St Nicholas's Day, boy bishops were elected in some cathedrals and parishes, and acted as bishops until 28 December, Holy Innocents' Day. Substantial presents were given and in many instances the money collected went to cathedral or church funds. At Great Dunmow there are two entries in Tudor Times of sums 'recevyd of the bysshop at Seynt Nicolas tyme'.

The custom was suppressed in 1541, revived three years later, and then again abolished.

In 1899, the Revd H.K. Hudson, vicar of Berden, Essex, started a modern version of the boy bishop ceremony in his parish, which continued until he left Berden in 1937.

As our stay was short, I shall only remark that the shops blazed with light, though the evening was dark, the lamps were so splendid, the streets so wide, it resembled taking a peep at Cheapside.

A visit to Colchester, winter 1778 (Anon.)

21 December is the winter solstice – the longest night and the shortest day. Wherever the wind is on this day, there it will stop for the next month. It is also St Thomas's Day; on this day old women went 'a-Thomasing' or collecting money.

In the fourteenth century the Forest of Essex was known as Waltham Forest (later Epping Forest). The dates for hunting in the forest were fixed: hart and buck from 6 July to 25 September, hind and doe from 25 September to Candlemas, the fox from Christmas to Lady Day, the hare from Michaelmas to midsummer, the boar from Christmas to Candlemas.

> If you wed in dull November
> Only joy will come, remember;
> When December snows fall fast,
> If you marry love will last.

Farmhouse near Colchester

The Ancient Roman saturnalia ran from 17 to 23 December, a festival of fire and light. In this country, the pagans celebrated the winter solstice and the birth of the sun, as from that day onwards the days began to lengthen and the power of the sun started to increase. The Gospels say nothing of the actual date of the birth of Christ and the early Church did not celebrate Christ's birth. Gradually the Nativity was celebrated on dates as widely apart as 1 and 6 January, 29 March and 29 September. It appears that it was Pope Julius (AD 337–52) who fixed the date as 25 December. However, Christians as well as pagans continued to celebrate the Winter solstice and the birth of the sun, but St Augustine instructed Christians to celebrate upon that day not the sun as pagans did but He who made the sun.

The Church also adopted some of the trappings of the pagan festival. Evergreens were the symbol of everlasting life, mistletoe, however, was not allowed in churches because of its strong pagan association with fertility.

In 1752 England abandoned the Julian Calendar and adopted the Gregorian Calendar, and with the loss of twelve days Christmas Day fell much earlier. It was a long time before country people came to accept it and many still believed Old Christmas Day (6 January) to be the true date. Snow is much more likely on 6 January than on 25 December and yet Christmas cards depict snow scenes, literature has snow at Christmas, and our thoughts are of snow on Christmas Day – 'a real old-fashioned white Christmas'. Yet since 1820 snow has fallen on Christmas Day only on twenty occasions, but there have been a few years with some snow before Christmas. In this century Essex has had only four really white Christmas Days.

Father Christmas is derived from St Nicholas and possibly Odin, the gift-bringer who rode the sky on an eight-legged

horse. He was first mentioned in a fifteenth-century carol which began: 'Hail, Father Christmas, hail to thee'. In 1644 Parliament abolished him and everything else connected with the feast of Christmas, including church services.

Carols, which were secular as well as religious, and not confined solely to Christmas, were also banned by the Puritans. For two hundred years they were not heard in churches or grand houses. Fortunately they were kept alive by simple and unlettered people; William Hone in 1826 called carols 'ditties which now exclusively enliven the industrious servant maid and the humble labourer'. Later the Victorians revived them in their desire for the traditional Christmas, and introduced some new carols as well as some 'new traditions'.

Boar's head was once the chief Christmas dish. Lesser dishes were goose, beef, lamb, or a pie composed of a variety of birds. Turkey did not come to England until the mid-sixteenth century.

Mince pies were known by the late sixteenth century and consisted of minced chicken, mutton, eggs, spices and raisins. To ensure twelve happy months in the following year, a mince pie should be eaten on each of the twelve days of Christmas.

Christmas puddings date from *c.* 1670. Earlier, plum porridge was eaten: a mixture of meat broth, fruit juice, breadcrumbs, raisins, spices and wine.

Christmas at Easton Lodge, Essex, was a time when all the employees (fifty house servants and one hundred outside workers), together with their families and children from the village school, gathered round a huge Christmas tree grown in

the park. Lady Warwick then distributed presents which included woollen jerseys, shawls and toys for the children.

During the very hard winter of 1895 she gave an extravagant ball at Warwick Castle and was rebuked by Robert Blatchford, editor of *The Clarion*, for 'idle junketing in a time of general misery'. She, in turn, went to Blatchford's office in order to rebuke him but returned home from their meeting in a thoughtful frame of mind and henceforth became an ardent worker for social reform.

In some districts on Boxing Day there was a ritual known as the Wren Hunt, but in Essex they said:

> The robin and the redbreast
> The robin and the wren,
> If ye go tak' out of the nest,
> Ye'll never thrive again.

Formerly, the Christmas season extended to Candlemas Eve (1 February) and home decorations were not taken down until this day. The belief that it is unlucky to leave decorations up after Old Christmas Day (6 January) is a comparatively modern superstition.

> If Candlemas Day be fair and bright,
> Winter will have another flight,
> If Candlemas Day be clouds and rain,
> Winter will be gone and will not come again.

Advertisement

DR MYLOCK PHEYARO

Doctor Mylock Pheyaro informs the Publick that he has removed from the King's Arms in Colchester to the Crown in Maldon, Essex, where he continues to cure (under the blessing of God) Cancerous Complaints, Fustulas, King's Evil, Ulcers in legs and other extremities, Scurvy breaking out in all parts of the Body, Pimples in the Face, St Anthony's Fire, Scald Heads, Itch, Gout, Rheumatism, and many other Disorders, too tedious to mention. What I have already done at Colchester, Manningtree, Wyvenhoe, Saxmundham, Woodbridge and Hadleigh in Suffolk, since June last, is a sufficient testimony of my ability, and those who need my assistance may, with good effect, through the help of God, apply to their friend and humble servant, Nov 1760.

Highwaywoman

HONE'S EVERYDAY BOOK

On the 24th November, 1735, a butcher near Romford, in Essex, was rode up to by a woman well mounted on a side saddle, who, to his astonishment, presented a pistol and demanded his money. In amazement he asked her what she meant, and received his answer from a genteel looking man, who coming to him on horseback, said he was a brute to deny the lady's request, and enforced this conviction by telling him that if he did not gratify her desire immediately he would shoot him through the head. The butcher could not resist such an invitation to be gallant, when supported by such arguments, and he placed six guineas and his watch in her hands.

Highwayman

LONDON EVENING POST

Essex produced Dick Turpin, the most famous highwayman of all time, but the legend owes far more to the fictitious account in Rickwood *by Harrison Ainsworth (1805–82) than to reality. Dick Turpin was born in 1704 at the Bull Inn, Hempstead. He became a butcher, then a smuggler at Canvey Island and a deer poacher in Epping Forest before becoming a highwayman. He and his gang were notorious for needless violence, and Turpin himself often kept carefully out of the way when his gang made the most dangerous raids. He never made the famous ride from London to York; that ride was accomplished by a highwayman known as Swift Nicks Nevison in 1724 when Turpin was apprenticed to a butcher in Whitechapel. Neither does Turpin appear to have done anything spectacular in Essex at Christmas time; in February 1735, however, the* London Evening Post *reported:*

On Tuesday night about 8 o'clock, five villains came to the house of Mr Lawrence, a farmer of Edgwaresbury, near Edgware in Middlesex, but the door being bolted they could not get in, so they went to the boy who was in the sheephouse and compelled him to call the maid who opened the door, upon which they rushed in, bound the master, maid and one man-servant, and swore they would murder all the family if they did not discover their money, etc; they trod the bedding under foot, in case there should be money hidden in it, and took about £10 in money, linen, etc, all they could lay

their hands on; they broke the old man's head, dragged him about the house, emptied a kettle of water from the fire over him, and ravished the maid, Dorothy Street, using her in a most barbarous manner, and then went off leaving the family bound, locked the door and took the key with them.

In the Seventeenth Century

HUMPHREY PHELPS

Latton, New Year's Day, 1641 'two of the sayde ringers, namelye, Jeremye Reeve, servant to William Stracye of Latton aforesayde, yeoman, and William Skynner, sonne to Widow Skynner of the sayde towne, did from the belfreye repaire to the Communion table in the Chancell of the sayde church, and in the sight of this Informant, as hee was standing in the belfreye, pull down the rales from about the sayde Table with theire hands. And sayeth that hee this Informant goeing out into the Churchyard did see the sayde Reeve and Skynner together with Henry Wennell, apprentice to John Starkys of the sayde Latton Potter, and one Henry Vinton, servant to one, Poole, a dish turner of the same, bringing the sayde rules out of the Chancell into the

Churchyard and from thence throwe them over the Churchyard wall into the Highwaye. And hee further sayeth that hee did see the sayde persons carrye the sayde broken rules neare to the whipping post of that towne, and there set them on fire.'

A carpenter was 'at the drinkeing of the sayde beere, and payed for part thereof. and that they did send for it to releeve theire necessities.'

The ringers 'did laye their moneyes together to the summe of two shillings, and sent Wennell for beere. And they sayde Wennell brought a Kilderkin, or such like vessell of beere, for the sayde moneye from the Black Lyon, an alehouse in Harlowe, on his shoulders, and sett it downe neare the Highe waye, where the rales were fired. And hee, the sayde Skynner, further sayeth that the sayde vessell was carryed thence (but he knoweth not by whome) into the

Colchester Castle has the largest keep in Europe, and is built mainly of Roman bricks

sayde Church porch, where the greater part of the sayde beere was dranke by them, the other Examinats, and divers others. And sayeth, that Henrye Vinton above sayde did carrye it into the Church, and into the belfrye, where the remainder was dranke up by themselves and the ringers. And hee lastlye sayeth, that the reason of his so pulling downe the rales was, because theye gave offence to his conscience, and that the placeing of them was against Gods lawes and the Kings: as appeareth by the twentyeth chapter of Exodus, and about the twentyeth verse: and lastlye because the rales had been pulled downe in other places without punishment therefore. And this Examinat lastlye sayeth that he, and the sayde other persons had no weapons at all, or anye offensive matter about them: and is verye sorye for his sayde offence, and confesseth it was most inadvisedlye done. And this Examinat doth not knowe of anye other persons counselling, countenancing or assisting thereunto.'

24 December 1652. 'Parliament spent some Time in Consultation about the Abolition of Christmas-day, pass'd Orders to that Effect, and resolv'd to sit on the following Day, which was commonly called Christmas-day.'

25 December 1655. 'There was no more notice taken of Christmas day in churches. . . . Cromwell's proclamation was to take place, that none of the Church of England should dare either to preach or administer Sacraments, teach school, etc, on pain of imprisonment or exile. So this was the mournfullest day in my life that I had seen.' (John Evelyn)

Although the Puritans were powerful in Essex, the people of Essex were not prepared to forego the Christmas festivities

altogether. The inhabitants of Hornchurch, for example, 'pay the great tithes on Christmas Day, and are treated with a Bull and Brawn. The Bull's Head is wrestled for. The poor have the scraps'. (Philip Morant (1700–70), Essex clergyman and author of *The History of Essex*)

Little work was done on farms on the days after Christmas and there was time for merriment. The festivities continued until Twelfth Night.

From the Barrington account books, Hatfield Broadoak:

To my Lady for Wassellers and the Morris dancers	5s
Given to the fellow that daunced with the Hobbyhorse	1s
To my Lord Illrule	5s
To the boys that showed tricks at Christmas	1s 6d
Given to the fidlers on Christmas Day	1s
Given to ye poore this Christmas	£3 9s 10d

Money was also given to musicians from Takeley and Epping. Bands, fiddlers and singers went round the streets and visited the gentry singing carols. (This is at variance with some records which state that no carols were heard in great houses for two hundred years since the Puritans' ban.) Gratuities were given by the Barringtons to waits from as far away as Colchester and Newmarket.

December 1854

HUMPHREY PHELPS

ANNUAL MEETING OF CHELMSFORD CO-OPERATIVE COAL SOCIETY, FOUNDED 1846.

The final closing of the doors of the Black Boy Hotel, Chelmsford, which for centuries has offered welcome to all travellers before the rail-road had sent post-horses to the dogs and stage coaches into obscurity . . . the old Black Boy thus falling victim to that meddling science which must needs invade the traffic of the turnpike road and convert steam into a common carrier . . . it was here that Margaret Catchpole halted with her celebrated horse on her way from Ipswich to Smithfield Market; and in one of the rooms of this hotel did that excellent man Dr Taylor sleep the night before he was burnt on Aldham Common, near Hadleigh.

Essex Poultry Show. The entries for this show, which is to take place at Colchester on the 28th, 29th and 30th inst., exceed 750 pens against 216 last year and, with the exception of Birmingham (now holding) will be the largest show in the kingdom.

The Essex and Suffolk Foxhounds will meet on Tuesday, 26th at Ardleigh Street.

Christmas Shopping

ETHELIND FEARON

Ethelind Fearon once said she was born in Victoria's reign and had never got over it. She also said she was unsympathetic with practically all modern trends and disliked hustle and big business. Claiming to be fundamentally lazy, she invented ways of dodging most work which was distasteful – especially writing. The late Mrs Fearon lived and farmed near Thaxted.

As it was Christmastime I had a great many other things on my mind. Puddings were done and, except the one which got burnt, they looked grand, but there was still the cake to ice. Pantomime rehearsals in the church hall were assuming some kind of reason and coherence instead of having the appearance of a village schoolmistress trying to teach a lunatic asylum Euclid and becoming involved in a civil war instead.

'Count thirty after he says "in the cupboard" and then open the door, Dolly. No, not *that* side; you'll knock him over. You come in *left*.' 'Your cue is "pots and pans", Mrs Fearon. Mind you drop the whole lot at once.' 'Frankie, when will you remember to enter on the word "crazy"?' 'Mrs Bailey, why can't I have a speaking part if my sister has? I'm only in the chorus.'

'A count of fifteen after the herald knocks is long enough. But don't *pant* so hard or we shan't hear what he says.'

'And when you hear Buttons say "dancing with the Prince", Mrs Fearon, ding the gong twelve times.' Which is a very monotonous job, and when I'd dung it about seven I'd lose count, or lose the rhythm or make one ding louder than the other so that it sounded as if we had a *most* erratic clock. No one would believe that gong-dinging was so complicated a matter, but it is practically a job for an expert and Mrs Bailey the producer had to install a metronome before I could turn out a really steady and mechanical midnight.

'I don't think the part of fairy godmother suits me, and I can't *bear* the sight of rats.'

'If Marcia has to fight with me as the second Ugly Sister *do* tell her to cut her nails.'

'Why must Zobie de Cinderella. No one could call her a *nice* girl.'

'We simply *must* work in a chorus. There's that lot we had left over from the *Trojan Women* you know, most of the hockey team really, and they'll be terribly offended if we leave them out again this time. They've got their costumes – snow boots cross-gartered with tape, old sheets and laurel leaves, and if they do a bit of conga-ing and a bit of Swan Laking and a bit of minuetting it'll break things up nicely.'

Edward, who was unfortunately present, said he reckoned that *that* hockey team would break up practically anything within sight, and what were we doing about reinforcing the stage?

But I promised to add six yards of white net and some spangles to my Christmas shopping list for the godmother's dress and left them discussing the possibility of making a wand by dipping a stick first in glue, then in Epsom salts, which are said to glitter. And Edward brooded all the way home on how he could make a pumpkin from papier mâché which should be large enough to hold Zobie's fairy coach (a child's push-chair) and fall apart to disclose it when whacked by the aforementioned wand.

CHRISTMAS SHOPPING

Which was quite a headache to him, but he had volunteered to be Gadgets Man and said airily that *anybody* can make pumpkins, and rather than eat his words he spent roughly twelve hours a day experimenting and was quite unliveable with until the job was done.

My shopping was no light matter either. Everyone said take a list, because without it I would quite certainly forget everything I wanted, and I still maintain that with a list and ten pounds any able-bodied woman *should* be able to buy presents for twelve people. But she can't, of course; I've tried it and I know.

'I will go up one side of Oxford Street and down the other,' I decided. Not that this prevented me from tacking like a ship in a gale from one side to the other, but it is nice to have a plan even if you don't stick to it, and things across the road always look so much better than what you have close to hand.

Though on inspection they prove to be identical. Which is the way of a lot of other things in life, too.

Superficially the shops were full, and scintillating with the most desirable objects, though with rather more Perspex cigarette boxes than were strictly necessary. But under scrutiny they fell into three main categories – too expensive, too poor in quality, or quite unsuitable for anyone on my list, which didn't seem to be so outrageous when I compiled it, but was regarded by most of the shop ladies with withering unsympathy.

> Sheepskin slippers size 12 for Grandfather.
> Green velvet slippers for Aunt Edith.
> Fleecy pink bedsocks for Aunt Dora.
> Pretty pink velvet dressing-gown for Sally.
> Silk shirt for Edward.
> Dog on wheels for Andrew.
> Bottle of Chanel perfume for Helga.
> Chamois waistcoat for Jonathan.
> Gloves for Nancy.
> Net for fairy queen.
> Hankies for Zobie's eldest child who *will* come to rehearsals and sniff.
> Christmas decorations.

I didn't exactly *see* any sheepskin slippers in the window, but there might be some inside the very glamorous emporium.

There were not. They suggested that perhaps I could make some myself. I might if I had a sheep, but I hadn't.

'The green velvet bedroom slippers then?' I asked. No. They had gold tissue evening sandals with heel-less heels and toeless toes, if you know what I mean, but they didn't look at all like Aunt Edith, even ignoring the fact that they were

seventy-nine shillings and elevenpence. Of any more hopeful ones 'the day's quota' was already exhausted. The young lady said they had some *too* amusing hair combs for a 'swept-up' style, or could she show me some Perspex cigarette boxes? But Aunt neither swept-up nor smoked, so we transferred our attention to pretty pink velvet dressing-gowns. Or to the department where they *might* have been.

Handkerchiefs for a child then? 'Ten-and-elevenpence for four in a box.' I explained that it wasn't that kind of child. Just one that I didn't know very well or like very much, but felt they'd be suitable because her nose was so runny. But they are still ten-and-elevenpence. Never mind. Try somewhere else; the day was young yet.

There happened to be an outfitter on the direct route, but his only silk shirts were a kind of stockinette stuff in navy or green, things which I have seen on a football field or a race-course, but nowhere else. Edward would not be grateful and would not hesitate to say so.

Thus far my money was still intact. If I hadn't gained, at least I hadn't lost anything.

Never mind, the day was *still* young and here was a gigantic toy department where Andrew's dog on wheels might well be lurking in wait for me among hundreds of Perspex objects which I feared were cigarette boxes.

Toys were plentiful, much better in quality and quantity than last year, and, alas, even more expensive. A bear on wheels was ten guineas, a plush Polar bear on his own paws three, a scooter five, a model aeroplane six, a rocking-horse of mean size fourteen, a pedal motor car fifteen, and jig-saw puzzles a pound. And the dolls had all gone plastic.

This was all very sad. Somehow a plastic doll is cold and uncuddly. The year before the war I bought a three foot Teddy Bear for a pound, a large and furry dog on wheels (still in use) for twenty-two shillings and sixpence, a 'Grand Prix' sort of

car for four pounds, and a rocking-horse as big as a real pony for four pounds ten shillings. Their counterparts either did not exist that Christmas, or were only for the children of millionaires.

Perhaps I should fare better in the stationery department, buying decorations for the Christmas tree, but even these were fantastic. There were coloured festoons at five shillings and ninepence each; sparkling silver-paper ornaments at half a guinea, and Christmas tree decorations at four shillings a time. I retired into a corner to indulge in some mathematics, and calculated that it would cost seven pounds ten shillings to festivate the drawing-room, or nineteen pounds two shillings if we included the wooden Christmas tree in a pot, its angular arms wrapped in green wool offered by one store.

I renounced them all and resolved to make do with an old wallpaper pattern book and some gum.

That was the fifth shop, but I was not beaten yet, not by a long way, though the day was not now *quite* so young. There were more people than I ever saw in one street before, and we all had to move the same way at the same time. Most of them were too wide, and carrying the more cornery kind of parcel. I regarded with satisfaction my so far untrammelled state, and turned into another store.

'Slippers, handkerchiefs, pretty pink velvet, etc' 'No, but we have Perspex cigarette boxes, paste bracelets at eighteen guineas, handbags at ten, fur gloves at seven, or French kid at three, perfume at five, and imitation pearls at eight.' And even the perfume wasn't Chanel, it was Worth's 'My Sin' or Bourjois' 'Evening in Paris', neither of which I felt quite expressed Helga's personality.

Nothing for a mother with ten pounds and twelve people to please.

Christmas Poultry Market

S.L. BENSUSAN

S.L. Bensusan, who lived at Langham, wrote more than five hundred tales and sketches of the Essex marshlands. The first appeared in 1898, the last shortly after his death in 1958 at the age of eighty-six. Rudyard Kipling, who admired Bensusan's marshland stories, said they would stand as a record 'when all agriculture is run by gentlemen and ladies out of London offices'.

Market Waldron poultry market on the following day provided all comers with a sensation. Elsewhere bullocks were a fair trade, dairy cows were moderate, calves fair, and pigs not so bad. But in the poultry market, where only 140 birds were penned, there was a veritable boom. Aged roosters that only seven days before had averaged three shillings and threepence were hard to buy at nine or ten; hens, long past laying, went up to twelve; geese made sixteen to eighteen; and three or four turkeys touched thirty-five shillings. A pen of six Rhode Island Red pullets in splendid condition actually fetched six guineas; and four fine white Sussex were withdrawn at four pounds, the auctioneer remarking that the reserve had not been reached.

Rumour, full of tongues, spread from one end of the market to the other. Mr Caplin had been heard to say that he feared

there was no living for the trade in such prices, but the breeder was now in the saddle, and would remain there till after Christmas. It was said that several buyers who had arrived late had been unable to get a single bird, so keen the demand, so high the price. Mr Mince was also overheard. He had said that, but for heavy contracts that he must fulfil whatever the loss, he would not attend the market next week. A dozen farmers' wives, who, hoping against hope, had sent a few birds into the market, were all nods and becks and wreath'd smiles. They congratulated one another on their discernment.

In the private room of the Cat and Fiddle, Mr Caplin, who had bought the six Rhode Island Reds, made a cash adjustment with Mr Mince, promising to leave the birds with him on the way home, and tossing double or quits for the agent's commission. Each was, however, a little heavy at heart.

The Christmas Poultry Sale at Market Waldron is always a striking feature. The auctioneers, Messrs Trudge and Baffle (established 1854), are noted for their generosity, and every year they offer £4 in prizes on the occasion; the first for the best turkey weighing over 35 lb; the second for the best table fowl weighing over 10 lb; the third for the best goose; and the fourth for the best basket of eggs. The first two prizes cannot always be claimed, and while Mr Baffle grows the best geese in the district, the manager, Mr Crake, is a specialist in the keeping of poultry under the intensive system.

But it was not for honour, or glory, or prizes that Maychester, and the Mudfords, and Nutting, and Meadowbank, and Gander's End, and Gallow's Green, and Tye Common, and Nasing Fichet sent their birds to the poultry pens in Market Waldron.

It was rather in the certain knowledge that there was a serious shortage in home supplies, a falling off in foreign shipments, and a growing demand for the simple luxuries of life, following upon the establishment of a stable Government.

The hopes of the poultry-raising community were not dashed, at least not until genuine buyers, who put in an early appearance, had retired hurt. For the satisfaction of their urgent needs they were compelled, very properly, to pay high prices; though, by one of those curious accidents that will arise, the early pens for the most part contained birds belonging to gentlemen not wholly unconnected with the ring. Then, for some reason which none shall interpret lightly, a silence, a listlessness, fell upon the company. Prices languished. They did more. They declined perceptibly, even rapidly. Hope had told too flattering a tale. In vain Mr Crake rallied the crowd, in vain he denounced his patrons and threatened to cease from giving birds away, to close the market and go home. Yet he says these things with unction.

It was unfortunate that none of his admonitions was addressed to the members of the buying ring. It may be that, by reason of their quiet unobtrusive demeanour, he overlooked them. Only now and again, when some overweening stranger attempted to buy a bird, and the knights of the ring were satisfied that he was not acting for the owner but was a *bona fide* bidder, did they run him up and make him pay for his impudence.

Henwives looked agitated, perplexed, even tearful, but they are not vocal in emergency, nor would outcry have helped them. They were in the hands of a skilled and ruthless company, bent upon making up the losses of the week before and providing a little material for Christmas gaiety. It was a sad procession that scattered to the farms.

In the private room of the Cat and Fiddle, half-a-dozen earnest men met and compared notes. Then, with the aid of papers and figures, they held another little sale of eggs and poultry. Even when the extravagance of the preceding week had been wiped out there was a substantial balance to the credit of enterprise, industry and resource.

from

The Journals of Arnold Bennett

Arnold Bennett, the author of numerous novels and plays, bought Comargues, a Queen Anne house in the village of Thorpe-le-Soken, in 1913. He wrote his third Clayhanger novel here, and sold the house in 1920. The following extracts from his Journals *were written at Comargues. Arthur L. Humphreys was a partner in Hatchards, the booksellers. J.C. Squire, poet and critic, was a contributor to the* New Statesman, *formed in 1913 and of which Bennett was a director. Ravel was a composer and Walpole a prolific author; Rickards was a prominent architect; Doran was Bennett's American publisher.*

1913, Thursday, December 4
On Tuesday Arthur L. Humphreys came up to lunch, and to inspect my books with a view to a catalogue. . . . We took

him to Kirby-le-Soken, Walton and Frinton. . . . He said that he thought novels of today immensely superior to those of 20 years ago. He said that at Xmas, numbers of people made up their minds to buy 'Whitaker and one other book'. The other book might be a book of devotional verse. He said that novels more and more dominated the book market.

1913, Monday, December 8
J.C. Squire came on Saturday. Long hair, Jaegerishly dressed.

1913, Monday, December 13
Excursion to Ipswich, Saturday. Shops closed at 1 p.m. – at least all good ones except antiquaries. We went into three and bought a number of things. Ravel also. Walpole came in the afternoon. . . .

1913, Saturday, December 27
Rickards came on Christmas Eve. Doran came on Sunday morning. . . . I am now re-reading *The Way of all Flesh*. It stands it.

1914, Sunday, January 18
Barber's yesterday at Frinton. Read (chauffeur) said he had been there and that it was smart and clean, but lacked things. Behind tobacco shop. Long white curtains over window (clean) to hide back yard. Very small room. Very small fire. 3 marble basins with fitments. No antiseptic arrangements as far as I could see. Room cold. Sturdy small boy who opened door for me, knickers, apron (not clean); 'Shall you operate on me?' 'No, sir,' with a grin. Man doing shaving. No greetings from barber. Dirty apron and coat hanging up on wall. Array of mugs with sponges. I stood with back to fire and looked at *Daily Mirror*. Had not to wait long. Place looked clean but wasn't. Thick dust on gas-shades and many cobwebs. Chair too

high, a modern chair, which required footstool. I commented on height. Barber said: 'It's not high enough for me as it is. I always have to stoop.' I suggested footstool. He said, 'They do have them in some places.' I asked if business good. 'No, very short season.' A nice mild man, tall, badly shaven, baggy worn knees. But decent. No energy. Had to go out in middle to talk to customer about mending a pipe – 'Excuse me, sir.' Parted my hair on wrong side and badly. Shoved his sleeve in my eye. Didn't show me the back of my head. Doubtful towels. Indiarubber sponge. Price 10d. Still a decent chap.

1914, Wednesday, December 16
Concert in aid of National Fund by Frinton Choral Society last night at Frinton Exhibition Hall. Very bad music, especially the ballads – all appallingly dull. A madrigal by Beale, fine, badly sung. Also in a pot pourri of national airs, the air 'The Minstrel Boy' seemed a masterpiece. It is. Orchestral suite rotten. Two apparently professional female singers sang with some skill the most putrid things; their gestures and facial movements comic, but of course they are too close to the audience in these small halls. The ordeal is too much. Audience asked for a lot of encores, especially of the worst things that were freely given. The only fun in these affairs is comic remarks to your friends, and the examination of all these ingenuous English faces that are nevertheless so difficult to decipher. I imagine all the people in their homes, in natural poses. A few tolerably dressed women in the audience. But for the most part a frightfully inartistic audience, showing their lack of taste in everything except their reserved demeanour.

1914, Tuesday, December 22
. . . Today I heard firing at Sea which seemed to be like a battle, and not like firing-practice. The first time I have had

Rough sea at Frinton

this impression since the war began, though we have heard
firing scores of times. . . .

1914, Wednesday, December 30
Great storm on Monday night. We lost 5 trees. A large elm
blew across the road, broke telegraph wires, and broke
through the vicarage fence, and blocked the road all night.
While I was out at 10.30 p.m. inspecting, I heard another
tree crashing and fled. Old oak fell into the pond.

1914, Thursday, December 31
Mr F., maltster, with £200,000 worth of buildings and stock,
called with the secretary of his company as to order for
destruction of the whole thing in case of emergency. He of
course wanted a proper guarantee of compensation. His best
argument, however, was that a fire would block both the
railway and the high road to Harwich. Speaking of military
measures, he told me he had been to the Home Office, and
that there had actually been drawn up an order to prevent

certain things being imported into this part of the world, lest advantage might accrue to invading enemy. The order was never promulgated.

1915, Thursday, January 7
Dr H. called this afternoon in a great state of excitement: 'I've called about a most unpleasant thing. But I thought I ought to tell you,' etc. His news was that the village was seething with the news that R. was a pro-German, and taking advantage of his position as chauffeur to the military representative to transmit secret information as to English plans through his sweetheart, a German girl, to the German authorities. H. believed it or half-believed it.

1915, Friday, January 8
I wrote to the Police Inspector last night and he called to see me today. He said he was constantly having complaints about signalling et. all absurd. I told him that R. was engaged to an English girl and that the whole thing was idiotic. He said he had received a letter about it (signed) and had to make a few inquiries, but expected of course no result. A very decent sort.

1915, Tuesday, January 12
Captain Bath and Lieut. Way of Ammunition Column of W. Somersets billeted here yesterday, 40 horses in Dakins's yard. Bath told me a tale of a party of German officers who spent some time in his town, Glastonbury – I think last year – with a fleet of cars in which they went out every night. They had a field and pretended to be perfecting a process for getting petrol from peat. They showed some petrol stated to be so obtained. Then they departed suddenly and mysteriously. I asked: why all this? He said it was to reconnoitre the country. I asked why they should reconnoitre the country at night when they were free to do it in the daytime, but he had no

answer. Anyhow, he was fully persuaded that it was a great case of 'intelligence'.

1917, Sunday, December 23

Fiddling about all day with small jobs instead of tackling my *Daily News* article, 'Yesterday'. However, I began to get the ideas for it about 6.30 and I wrote it this morning in bed. . . .

Captain Hill and wife came last night. He related how after a long period (several weeks) of 'special vigilance' he was sleeping in a blanket on the floor of the gardener's cottage at Thorpe Hall when a despatch rider burst in just like a stage despatch rider, at 3 a.m. The despatch contained one word, which for Hill had no meaning. The rider couldn't tell him anything and only insisted on a signature in receipt, which of course Hill gave. Hill then got up and went to see another OC near. This OC had received the same message and also had not the least idea what it meant. Other CO's were afterwards found to be in the same case.

1917, Tuesday, December 25th

War. Only about half a pint of methylated spirits left in the house. Marguerite decided to keep this in stock for an emergency of illness, etc. Wise. So I can no longer make my own perfect tea at what hour I like in the morning. And this morning I had poor servant-made tea. However there is a hope of me getting some other heating apparatus.

1917, Wednesday, December 26

Only seven sat down to dinner last night, owing to difficulties of transport and engagements of officers for mess dinners. This is the smallest Xmas dinner we have had in this house. Soldiers were noisy outside during the day. Mason came for lunch and stayed till after nightfall. He rode off in falling snow, having made Richard a present of all the chemical

reagents which he had ordered for him. . . . Much bad music after dinner.

1918, Friday, January 11

Marguerite bought a pig at the end of the year. It was a small one, but we have been eating this damned animal ever since, in all forms except ham, which has not yet arrived. Brawn every morning for breakfast. Yesterday I struck at pig's feet for lunch, and had mutton instead. They are neither satisfying nor digestible, and one of the biggest frauds that ever came out of kitchens. All this is a war measure, and justifiable. I now no longer care whether I have sugar in my tea or not. We each have our receptacle containing the week's sugar, and use if how we like. It follows us about, wherever we happen to be taking anything that is likely to need sugar. My natural prudence makes me more sparing of mine that I need be. Another effect of war is that there is a difficulty in getting stamped envelopes at the P.O. The other day the postmaster by a great effort and as a proof of his goodwill got me £1 worth, which won't go far.

It occurred to me how the war must effect men of 70, who have nothing to look forward to. The war has ruined their ends, and they cannot have much hope.

At Tolleshunt D'Arcy, 1939

MARGERY ALLINGHAM

Margery Allingham lived at Tolleshunt D'Arcy. From the late 1920s until her death in 1966 she wrote a series of detective novels featuring Albert Campion, which gained world-wide fame. In 1940 she also produced a record of the village of Tolleshunt D'Arcy in wartime.

Christmas was the last of the feasts. There was talk about sacrifice and economy, but no real signs of it. The Wardens had given up waiting round for an attack that never came, and the Post had been transferred to the studio, although the sideboard was still full of boots. With the restoration of the dining-room much of normal home life returned, and in that, I think, our house was fairly typical of Auburn.

In the beginning a great many people had been in the habit of getting out their gas-masks and going downstairs on a raid warning; but now, as night after night went by with no interruptions, gradually things settled again and we were 'lulled into a false security', as the papers said afterwards so angrily, as if we had lulled them and not they us. Most of the evacuees had gone from the village, but there were still a few for whom we had been able to find houses of their own, although even these were beginning to wilt before the weather. Christine had nearly given up grieving after Tony,

who with one or two others had spent a long time with us while his sister was being born. She had also given up pouncing on me with a toothcomb every morning, and she and Margaret had ceased the nightly precautionary hunt in the kitchen.

The time was almost normal save for the ever-present underlying sensation of waiting, and, to be honest, a new sociability and life which had not been so apparent in the village before the great upheaval. We had all come out from behind our lattices a little, and I for one had found the experience rejuvenating.

The war still absorbed practically all our spare attention, but because of the great lid of secrecy and silence, which still almost alone among all the emergency measures appeared to be absolutely efficacious from the outset, it was not at all easy to get any vivid picture of the position anywhere. To most of us blindfold in Auburn, going about in much our usual way now that the first shock appeared to have been a false alarm, the situation in France, with the two armies facing one another in consolidated positions and a no-man's patrol ground in between, suggested a sort of new-fangled Somme with a certain amount of modern comfort for the troops. Poland was a horrible tragedy, a murder and a rape which could only be avenged and repaid when we could get at her; and meanwhile the magnificent Finns were setting our imaginations on fire and carving an example for Greece and us to follow, and we were eagerly expecting a Scandinavian entry into the war and a French and British Norseland expedition.

At that time, and again now I should say, real secrecy in war-time on the part of the Government usually suggests one thing to the ordinary person who has helped to put the reigning party in power and who believes in the Prime Minister, and that is that some important move to frustrate the enemy is being planned and put into execution. All these

generalisations of mine refer only to the rank and file of Auburn, and not to the students of the times or the folk who make a serious hobby of politics. Some of these people's ideas are even wilder and sometimes they are nearer the mark, but I can only hope to explain what it has all looked like from an ordinary point of view, like my own or, say, Sam's, or any other busy person's who has had his own urgent affairs to look after as well.

I thought the Government was working like a fiend to get ready for a smashing Spring offensive, probably in the north, and I thought we were incomparably better equipped, especially in the air, than we turned out to be. I thought that the reason I did not see any factories going up was because they were being built in safer places, and I thought workmen were not being called up faster because they were not needed. It never occurred to me that we were in such extraordinary danger.

Remembering what other people said at the time, I don't think I was alone.

At Christmas, therefore, we were sanguine enough. We were being given time, we imagined, to build up a colossal war machine, the Jerry seemed to be in no mind to attack us from the air, and it felt as though it was going to be all right to have a few mild celebrations after all.

For us at home it turned out to be a curious, Jane Austenish Christmas, involving two separate but exactly similar midday parties in the same week for the two halves of a Searchlight unit with whom P.Y.C. had made friends in Mr Spitty's pub, and who had been moved on to a bleak ploughed hillock close to our old house down the road to Bastion.

Cooee in khaki and Joyce, my younger sister, on leave from the Wrens, were anachronisms, but the spirit and atmosphere were ridiculously alike. The Terriers were mainly young and decorous in mixed company, as the young are in England

to-day in direct contrast to ourselves ten or fifteen years ago, and even more different from our immediate elders, the war survivors, who as a class have even now in full middle age a gift for playing the goat on festive occasions. They were both good parties, and there was a great deal of genuine jollity, a lot of eating and much martial thumping on the wood floors. The soldiers were living in uncomfortable and intolerably dull conditions, and yet with all the freedom and fun of being a gang of lads together. Their need was for formal civilisation instead of the reverse, as had hitherto been more common.

The weather, too, all that winter was old-fashioned and together with the petrol control, produced conditions which I had forgotten since I was a child. Probably it was this, the sudden return of distance, which was the first physical change after the brief return of the children which the war produced in Auburn. It gave me, at any rate, a most extraordinary sense of the untrustworthiness of time as anything but a convenient short-term gauge. When I was a child Bastion was a morning's journey away by buggy if the weather was good. Just before the war it was scarcely round the corner by car. Now it is a long slow bus journey, sometimes entailing a call in at Mudlarking out in the marsh. Time and distance have lost that constancy with which I used to credit them, and their falseness is found out. They depend on other things.

It was an unusual winter, though, for any age. Norry was roughing horses all day. The school bus had to turn back on the Fishling road several times. Birds froze on the trees, and the gulls, so lovely on the wing and so clumsy and out-of-drawing on their feet, came clamouring round the house for food.

In spite of the inconvenience, the frozen pumps and the burst pipes, the absence of papers and mail, there is a peculiar sense of safety and cosiness in this kind of crisis in a village

like Auburn. I used to feel the same thing very acutely when I was small in the hard, paraffin-lit winters of my youth. We could be comfortably marooned for days, safe from the terrors of boarding school, the horrors of the dentist, and from the fear of Granny being called away or a governess coming down. If Mr Whybrow, the carrier, could not get into Bastion on his weekly visits, we were cut off indeed and the situation approached the calamity stage which I always secretly enjoyed, being at that age and in private rather a one for calamities. However, I learnt then that to sit by a fire after battening down the house before a tearing blizzard off the sea and to listen to the frustrated howling of the elements is one of the great pleasures in life, one of the most precious fruits of a triumphant civilisation.

Seasonal Fare

HUMPHREY PHELPS

OYSTER SOUP FROM COLCHESTER

2 dozen oysters
3 oz flour
1 pint white stock
3 oz butter
1$^{1}/_{2}$ pints milk
cayenne pepper
1 teaspoonful anchovy sauce

Beard the oysters and blanch them in the white stock and make a roux of the butter and flour. When well blended add the oyster liquor and blend in the anchovy sauce and bring to the boil. Add the milk gradually and bring back to boiling point. Then add the cayenne pepper. Halve the oysters and strain the soup over them.

Oyster soup is best eaten with thin brown bread and butter and taken with stout.

EPPING SAUSAGES

3 lb lean pork
3 lb suet
1 lemon
pepper
$^{1}/_{2}$ teaspoon nutmeg

Butcher's Christmas display, Coggeshall, *c.* 1910

1–2 eggs
a generous pinch each of thyme, savory and marjoram
1 tablespoon chopped fresh sage
1 teaspoon salt

Combine the minced pork, herbs, suet, nutmeg, pepper, salt and grated lemon rind. Beat the eggs and mix to make the mixture soft enough to form into sausage shapes and fry gently in a very little fat.

DUNMOW CHITTERLING PASTIES

Make a quantity of shortcrust pastry, roll out and cut into circles for pasty cases. Mince up some small pigs chitterlings

and mix with minced apples, sugar and spice. Then lay generous heaps on the pasty cases, seal and bake in hot oven for about 20 minutes, then lower oven until the pasties are well cooked.

GOSFIELD PLUM PUDDING

$1/2$ lb each of shredded suet and sieved breadcrumbs
a pinch of salt
$1/2$ teaspoon each of ground ginger, grated nutmeg and mixed spice
$1/2$ lb raisins
$1/4$ lb mixed candied peel
1 oz Jordan almonds
4 beaten eggs
$1/2$ lb currants
$1/2$ lb castor sugar
$1/2$ gill brandy or rum

Mix together the suet, breadcrumbs, salt and spices. Add the raisins, chopped peel and chopped almonds, currants and sugar. Mix together with the eggs and brandy or rum. Line the base of a buttered medium pudding basin with buttered paper. Add the batter which should come to within an inch of the rim. Cover with buttered paper and then with a pudding cloth. Place in a saucepan of boiling water to reach halfway up the side of the basin. Cover with a lid and boil for about six hours then remove, making sure that the pudding cloth is still securely tied to form a handle and hang up in a dry airy place. Re-cook for about two hours on Christmas Day. Serve with a rich sherry sauce.

SECOND WORLD WAR CHRISTMAS PUDDING RECIPE

6 oz raisins
8 oz sultanas
8 oz carrots
2 oz candied peel (if available – grated carrot and mashed
   potato make a good substitute if not)
5 oz self-raising flour
5 oz fresh breadcrumbs
5 oz margarine
Grated rind and juice of 1 orange (if not available 1 heaped
   tablespoon of marmalade)
3 level tablespoons dried egg
1/4 pint milk
4 oz demerara or granulated sugar
2 tablespoons cider, beer, brandy or milk
1 heaped teaspoon mixed spice
1 level teaspoon cinnamon
1/2 level teaspoon nutmeg
pinch of salt

Rub margarine into flour. Mix all dry ingredients together.
Add liquid and mix well. Put into greased bains, tie down as
usual and boil for 4 hours.

SECOND WORLD WAR CHRISTMAS CAKE RECIPE
(without eggs)

$^1/_4$ lb plain flour
$^1/_2$ lb ground rice
$^1/_2$ lb granulated sugar
$^1/_2$ lb currants
$^1/_2$ lb mixed peel
$^3/_4$ lb butter or margarine
1 teaspoon bicarbonate of soda
12 drops almond essence
$^1/_2$ pint boiling milk

Mix the dry ingredients well. Boil the milk except for 1 tablespoonful, which should be mixed with the bicarbonate of soda. Boil the milk and butter together, then pour over the dry ingredients and beat well, then pour in the milk and bicarbonate of soda and beat again. Put into an eight inch well greased and lined tin and bake in a good oven for about 4 hours.

In the Second World War, food rationing was introduced on 8 January 1940. Each person per week was limited to 4 oz bacon, 12 oz sugar and 4 oz butter; and later 1/1d worth of meat (offal not rationed), 2 oz tea, 2 oz each of butter, margarine and cooking fat, 1 oz cheese. Many other foods were put on coupons. Food rationing did not end until 1954.

D'ARCY SPICE APPLE

This fine dessert apple variety was found in the gardens at The Hall, Tolleshunt D'Arcy *c.* 1785. For a period in the mid-nineteenth century, however, a nurseryman near Chelmsford marketed it under the name of Beddow Pippin. It is reputed

only to reach perfection when grown in Essex. The apple is coloured both green and yellow with some russet and has crisp flesh with an aromatic tang. A splendid apple for Christmas by which time it is at its best and, being a good keeper if properly stored, remains at its best until March.

WINTER ALE (formerly Christmas Ale)

Winter ale is brewed by T.D. Ridley & Sons Ltd at Hartford End Brewery, Chelmsford. This ale has an original gravity of 1050, dark brown in colour with a rich flavour and a fine

An advertisement for Ridleys Winter Ale

aroma. It is made from roasted East Anglian malt, Fuggles and Golding's hops. Winter ale is available from November to February. The brewery which stands beside the River Chelmer was built in 1842.

COLE'S TRADITIONAL FARE

A.J. Cole started a high-class bakery business at Great Chesterfield in 1939. The business prospered and moved to Saffron Walden, and in 1988, due to an increasing demand, it returned to Great Chesterfield to new and larger premises. Now known as Cole's Traditional Bakery Ltd, much of its success is due to its insistence upon traditional values and the use of only first-class ingredients. Many of the recipes date

A selection of Coles Traditional Christmas Puddings

back to the nineteenth century. All products are free from artificial colourings, flavourings and preservatives.

TIPTREE JAMS

Wilkins & Sons Ltd of Tiptree was founded in 1885. The founder A.C. Wilkin used to quote the seventeenth-century poet, Thomas Carew:

> No foreign gums nor essence fetched from far
> No volatile spirits nor compounds that are
> Adulturate, but at Nature's cheap expense
> With far more genuine sweets refresh the sense.

The high standards set by the founder have been maintained; the fruit is grown at Tiptree and no artificial flavourings or preservatives are used. In recent years Christmas puddings have been added to the wide range of quality products.

THE ESSEX PIG

Ham, no less than turkey, goose, plum pudding, mince pies and cake, is a feature of Christmas; and the county of Essex produced a breed of pig to provide the ham. It is said that the Essex is an indigenous breed, descended from the half-wild swine of the afforested and reeded Essex of the Middle Ages. By this century it had been much improved but was still thrifty and hardy. Unfortunately modern fashion has not favoured this once-popular breed and it has now merged with a very similar breed – the Wessex Saddleback – to become the British Saddleback.

Coaching Days

LEONARD P. THOMPSON

*Leonard Philip Thompson was born in Ipswich in 1907 and is
the author of several books. These two pieces are from* Suffolk
Coaching Days.

To travel by mail-coach was to enjoy several advantages. By
comparison with the stage-coaches they were fast and
comfortable. They were maintained at a high level of
efficiency and smartness, and an impressively uniformed and
well-armed guard ensured a degree of protection from
highwaymen which no stage-coach could guarantee. Not that
the pistol, sword and blunderbus which the guard carried was
intended for the protection of passengers; it was, first and
foremost, for the defence of His Majesty's Mails. At the same
time, this formidable armament with its implied threat of
certain death to any highwayman who should be so bold as to
attempt a mail robbery, had the desired effect of securing an
extensive degree of immunity from the attentions of the
'gentlemen of the road'.

The first of the East Anglian mail-coaches was that which
began to operate between London and Norwich in March,
1785. Six years were to pass, however, before Ipswich was
firmly established on a regular mail-coach route. At 2.30 p.m.
on May 30, 1791, the Royal Mail Coach, by way of Ipswich to
London, set out on its first journey from the Great Yarmouth
Mail Coach Office at the Star Tavern on the Quay. It reached
the White Horse, Fetter Lane, at 8 o'clock the next morning.

It was advertised to leave this famous London coaching inn at 6 p.m. each day, and reach Yarmouth 'by dinner time next day'. In its early days, this coach carried four inside and four outside passengers, but the 'outsides' were later reduced to two.

On the 'up' journey, the Mail travelled by way of Lowestoft, Wangford and Yoxford, where it stopped at the Tuns. A mail diligence operating from this inn maintained a postal link with Halesworth and Beccles.

At Ipswich, the Mail stopped at the Great White Horse Hotel, where passengers supped. The Fleece at Colchester was reached at midnight; horses were changed and mail bags picked up – a procedure that was repeated just three hours later, when the 'down' coach called.

SHAVE'S COACHES
FOR CHRISTMAS AND NEW YEAR'S DAYS

Shave's Yarmouth and Beccles Coach (for those days) will set out from the Dukes Head, on the Quay, Yarmouth, early on Friday mornings, 22nd and 29th December, and from the King's Head, Beccles, at 6 o'clock, calling at the Angel – Halesworth, Tuns – Yoxford, Bell – Saxmundham, White Hart – Wickham Market, Crown – Woodbridge, two hours before their usual time in the proper rotation, to the Coach Office, Brook Street, Ipswich, and from thence, early on Saturday morning to the Saracens Head, Aldgate, in proper time for the porters to deliver parcels and presents that evening to the extreme parts of the town.

The Ipswich and Colchester Post-Coach from the Office on the Cornhill, Ipswich, to the Four Swans, Bishopsgate, London, will set out on Saturday mornings the 23rd and 30th at four in the morning.

The Coaches return from the above Inns on Christmas Day at the usual times.

This advertisement, which appeared in the *Ipswich Journal* on Saturday, December 16, 1786, was one of the many such announcements which were a regular feature of that newspaper throughout the whole of the coaching age. Shave was a recurring name in those advertisements during the second half of the eighteenth century, for the Shave family played an important part in establishing various road travel services to link Suffolk and Essex with London.

The business was founded by Thomas Shave, whose wagon, in 1741, left Ipswich for Colchester every Monday, and returned the following day. His business developed, and by 1750 he was operating stage-coaches between Woodbridge and Colchester. Meanwhile, the carrying side of the Shave concern was developed by his son, also Thomas, and by 1758 he had extended the service to cover a wagon trip of just over 100 miles between Saxmundham and London. By 1766, Thomas Shave had gone into partnership with Charles Harris, and they ran fast coaches from the Great White Horse in Ispwich to Colchester. By the closing years of the eighteenth century, Thomas Shave had become a coach operator of considerable significance and affluence. From his premises on Cornhill, Ipswich, he was running a daily coach to London, a coach to Yarmouth three times a week from the coach office in Brook Street, and – from the same starting place – a heavy coach three times a week to London.

At Christmas

THOMAS TUSSER

At Christmas play and make good cheer,
For Christmas comes but once a year.

*Thomas Tusser was born at Rivenhall, near Witham, Essex.
An an early age he was sent to Berkshire to serve as a
chorister, and later he went to St Paul's Cathedral and
thence to Eton College. Eventually he married and became a
farmer at Cattawade on the Essex border where he became
the first to introduce barley into England. At Cattawade,
in 1557, he began to write a sound treatise on farming –*
The Hundred Good Pointes of Husbandrie – *which
was later expanded to* Five Hundred Pointes *as well as* A
Hundred Good Pointes of Huswifery. *Unfortunately he
was unable to practice what he preached and his farming
was a failure.*

*Tusser was the originator of very many proverbs and sayings
although few are credited to him today.*

DECEMBER'S HUSBANDRY

O dirty December,
For Christmas remember.

When Frost will not suffer to dike and to hedge,
then get thee a heat, with thy beetle and wedge:

Once Hallowmas come, and a fire in the hall,
such slivers do well for lie by the wall.

Get grindstone and whetstone for tool that is dull,
or often be letted, and fret belly-full:
A wheel-barrow also be ready to have,
at hand of thy servant, thy compas to save.

Give cattle their fodder in plot dry and warm,
and count them for miring, or other like harm:
Young colts with thy wennels together go serve,
lest lurched by others, thy happen to serve.

Christmas is coming, the geese are getting fat. . . .

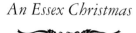

CHRISTMAS HUSBANDLY FARE

Good husband and huswife, now chiefly be glad,
things handsome to have, as they ought to be had.
They both do provide, against Christmas do come,
to welcome their neighbors, good chere to have som(e).

Good bread and good drinks, a good fier in the hall,
brawne, pudding, and souse, and good mustarde withal.
Biefe, mutton, and Porke, and good Pies of the best,
pig, veale, goose, and capon, and turkey wel drest,
Chese, apples, and nuttes, and good Caroles to hear,
as then, in the cuntrey is counted good cheare.

from JANUARY'S HUSBANDRY

When Christmas is ended, bid feasting adieu,
go play the good husband, thy stock to renew,
Be mindful of rearing, in hope of a gain,
dame profit shall give thee reward for thy pain.

Who both by his calf and his lamb will be known,
may well kill a neat and a sheep of his own.
And he that can rear up a pig in his house,
hath cheaper his bacon, and sweeter his souse.

PLOUGH MUNDAY

Plough Munday, the next after Twelftide be past,
biddeth out with the plough, the worst husband is last.
If Ploughman get hatchet or whip to the skreene,
maydes loseth their Cocke if no Water be seen.

Tea Party

ETHELIND FEARON

This, like 'Christmas Shopping', is an extract from Most
Happy Husbandman, *published in 1946.*

Marian has been concocting the essentials for a Christmas tree. All the boiled eggs for weeks have been opened with delicate precision and treasured like Dresden china. More so. When there were sufficient for her purpose she painted them from a motley collection of little tins which held repulsive oddments of bright enamel, gold paint and hideous orange lacquer. With a bright string hung through the end they are tied, open end downwards, to the Christmas tree and look like fairy-tale bells, all little dabs of purple and blue and gold merged in rainbow hues.

The enemy has been kind enough to shower us with bushels of tinfoil in streamers, a gift straight from heaven which is eagerly collected and hung in dingle-dangles from the ends of the branches, although probably not intended for that purpose.

The tree itself is a beautiful young fir dug up from the plantation, roots and all, and planted in a huge flower pot. After Twelfth Night it will be carefully replanted in its old place to dig in its toes again and go on growing. It looks lovely when Jonathan has been called in to fix the electric lights, which twinkle like incandescent appendices in red and green. Spreading its dark arms against the panelling it bears the silvered icicles of German foil dripping from bough to

bough, and little shimmery globes of many-coloured fire which were our breakfast eggs a week or two ago.

This time there will be no present for Samuel the cat. Last year we tied a chicken leg on the topmost branch for him, alongside the fairy, and on Christmas eve he climbed up while the house was sleeping and stole it prematurely.

Marian says he's so pretty when he steals (with an absentminded air, and both eyes shut) that she is obliged to forgive him anything, even her breakfast kidney. It is perhaps as well that we have no women judges if that is their outlook on thieving.

The last of the ploughing is done and the earth left to the elements for the final breaking-down. The last leaf has fallen, and rooks cluster like black pears in the topmost branches of the naked elms.

Draining, ditching, threshing and a dozen other jobs are under way. People say '*What* can anyone find to *do* in the country in the winter.'

If you're producing something – anything – there is always enough to do. The country is never dull, although a dull mind can make it so.

We work. And when work is done we rest. We eat and drink and talk and go to bed. Some of us get born and a few of us die. And that's all.

It doesn't sound a lot and yet somehow put together it is a lifetime, and if we've missed anything we don't notice it.

Every December, just before Christmas, we organise a teaparty in the village hall for the old age pensioners. There is a Christmas tree with some kind of little present for everyone, and such a profusion of cakes, jellies, mince pies, sausage rolls and blancmanges that a stranger would suppose we were entertaining refugees.

After tea they always have a concert to which anyone in the village may come by paying a shilling as they walk in, a similar amount being handed to each ancient on going out, so that the two processes more or less cancel out.

The programme is much as usual this year. Tea at half-past five, presents handed down from the tree by Sandy, thinly disguised as Father Christmas, at half-past six, concert at seven.

Marian as usual is at the piano, an ancient upright with the peculiar hollow tinkle common to pianos in village halls. She dearly loves a tune, the commoner the better, and can play anything with equal ease either facing the piano or looking over her shoulder to see if the singer is going through the chorus three times or only twice. Besides, she knows where the three dumb notes are and can dodge them, whereas a better player might be completely flummoxed by such a trivial deficiency. I have noticed that the more one is an expert, the more easily is he confounded by the unexpected obtrusion of the primitive.

I am, as usual, the Man who Moves Things, a handyman, lurking in the dark recesses behind the stage, to produce tables and chairs as required, disgorge cutlery for the inevitable Stage Breakfast, tend the slightly intractable curtain, and be there when wanted, but otherwise as far out of the way as possible.

Talent is strictly parochial, the same old performers singing the same old songs they have done these many years. Any innovation would be slightly disconcerting to the audience who would feel that they were being left behind and couldn't join in.

Mrs Potton has volunteered to sing, a proceeding which I regard with some misgiving, fearing that she may introduce an over-opulent note into an entirely domestic atmosphere. But even though I doubt her wisdom I cannot refuse the offer.

A Christmas party at a children's home, Saffron Walden, 1960

Boy George is the only performer from the farm. He renders 'Land of Hope and Glory' on a cornet with slightly too much spit and a certain amount of groping for top notes, but stays the course nobly, and finishes up with a burst of speed and loud acclamations from the multitude in the body of the hall.

Tiny Caton need only be himself. Wearing his grandfather's smock, buskins, beaver hat and red handkerchief, he sings farming songs, to the glory of the naïve nature and essential shrewdness of the Essex labourer.

His dialect is superb, his make-up just bucolic enough and

not too much. I could listen to him for hours. It's funny all right, uproariously funny, but it's more than that, there's something elemental about it that goes right to the heart of the labouring life.

He is succeeded by our comedy trio, whose sketch the audience know so well that they join in. If a player goes astray they render kindly assistance.

Voice from the rear, "Old 'ard a minnit, Jack, you've forgot the bit about the burnt saussage'.

'Right you are, boy,' says Jack from the stage, 'I bin an' forgot it agin same as usual. Thank yer from me.' And he knuckles his forehead in gratitude, goes back to pick up the dropped line, and proceeds smoothly on his way again.

Two girls sing a duet. One of them, stricken dumb in the middle of the verse, can do nothing but coyly search the corners of the ceiling for inspiration, one leg wrapped round the other and hands behind back in an agony of shyness, while the other valiantly carries on, but in the second verse her mate revives somewhat and gets through half of it without moving her mouth, a marvellous feat.

Mrs Potton is the next performer. From my peephole in the back curtain I can't quite see her as she walks on, but the cheering and stamping surprise me considerably. I had not believed her to be so popular.

And then the reason becomes apparent. Ample of architecture, and florid of hue, she struts the stage in an extravagant paraphrase of bull-fighting attire. Black satin breeches caress her ample thighs, a scarlet cummerbund and yellow blouse delineate her convexity all too unkindly, a broad black felt crowns saucily her coal black curls, and behind the left ear lurks a paper rose.

I am deprived of half the effect, but if the front view is anything like as funny as the rear she is doing pretty well. The audience laps it up and will not be quiet, and I instantly

revoke all my previous decisions about her. If she is human enough to make of herself a Roman holiday for the assembled ancients, God bless her, she'll do!

But, presently, by much waving of an over-diamonded hand, she achieves silence, and explains with a kind of pained resignation that she isn't funny at all. She is a bull-fighter who loves a little gipsy, and is going to sing a song about it.

Conundrum

ANON.

Christus Natus Est the Cock
Croweth to the lazy clock.
Christus Natus Est he crows;
Christus – and the Raven knows,
And the lambs, as you shall hear.
Loudly croweth Chanticleer,
With an eager, piercing sound,
To the beasts that lie around;
And they question and reply,
While the Sun mounts up the sky.
Quando? Quando? and again –
That's the Duck who's asking when?
In hac nocte the Raven croaks
From the old snow-laden oaks.

Quando? Quando? from beyond
The willows by the frozen pond
In hac nocte croaks the Raven
From the bare winter's haven
Ubi? Ubi? Listen there –
That's the Bull who's asking where?
In Bethlehem the Lambs do Bleat,
And seek their dams with happy feet.
Ubi? Ubi? the bull lows,
Standing black against the snows;
And the Lambs in Bethlehem;
It was God who told it them.

Lost Sheep

S. BARING-GOULD

Sabine Baring-Gould, the author of Onward Christian
Soldiers *and over one hundred and fifty books, including some
novels, was rector of East Mersea from 1871 to 1881. The
following is from his novel* Mehalah, *a story of the Essex salt
marshes, which was published in 1880. The story, although set
in the 1820s, probably reflects Baring-Gould's time at East
Mersea, and shows an interesting and presumably accurate
report of the coastal attitude towards Christmas and the New
Year.*

It was Christmas Eve. A hard frost had set in. The leaves which had hung on the thorn trees on the Ray rained off and were whirled away by the wind and scattered over the rising and falling waters in the Rhyn. On the saltings were many pools, filled from below, through crab burrows, from the channels; when the tide mounted, the water squirted up through these passages and brimmed the pools, and when the tide fell, it was sucked down through them as if running out of a colander. Now a thin film of ice was formed about the edges of these pondlets, and the marsh herbs that dipped in them were encased in crystal. The wild geese and ducks came in multitudes, and dappled the water of Mersea channel.

'There's four gone,' said Abraham Dowsing in a sulky voice to Mehalah.

'Four what?'

'Four ewes, to be sure; out of what else have we more than one?'

'Where are they?'

'That is what I should like to know. Two went yesterday, but I said nothing about it, as I thought they might be found, or that I hadn't counted aright; but there's two more missing to-day.'

'What can have become of them?'

'It's no use asking me. Is it like I should know?'

'But this is most extraordinary. They must have wandered off the saltings, on to the causeway, and so got away.'

'That is likely, ain't it,' said Abraham. 'It is like the ways of sheep, to scatter, and two or three to go off and away from all the flock. I'll believe that when sheep change their nature.'

'They must have fallen into a pool and been drowned.'

'Then I should find their carcases; but I haven't. Perhaps there has been a spring tide at the wrong time of the year and overflowed and drowned them. That's likely isn't it?'

'But Abraham, they must be found.'

'Then you must find 'em yourself.'

'Where can they be?'

'I've told you it is no use asking me.'

'Can they have been stolen?'

'I reckon that is just about it.'

'Stolen!' exclaimed Mehalah, her blood flashing to her face and darkening cheek and brow. 'Do you mean to tell me that some scoundrel has been here in the night, and carried off four of our ewes?'

Abraham shrugged his shoulders. 'Mud tells tales at times.'

'Hark!' she said, 'the Christmas bells.'

Faint and far off could be heard the merry pealing of the Colchester bells. The wind had shifted.

'Peace on earth and good will to men,' muttered Elijah; 'But to them that fight against their destiny fury and hate.'

'Go back Elijah and speak to me no more on this matter. I will not hear you again. I have but endured it now.'

'This is Christmas Eve,' said Rebow. 'In eight days is the New Year, and then you will be in Red Hall, Glory!'

No more sheep were stolen; but then the moon was filling her horns, and a robbery could not be committed without chance of detection. But though nothing further had been taken, Mehalah was uneasy. Some evilly disposed person had visited the Ray and plundered her and her mother of four ewes; others, or the same, might attempt the house, in the hopes of finding money there. The auction had shown people that Mistress Sharland was not without money.

On New Year's Eve Mehalah went to Colchester to make some purchases for the New Year. The kalends of January and

not the Nativity of Christ is the great winter festival among the Essex peasantry on the coast. They never think of wishing one another a Happy Christmas, but only a Merry New Year. No yule log is burnt, no mummers dance, no wassail bowl is consumed at Christmas, but each man who can afford it deems himself bound to riot and revel, to booze and sing, to wake the death of the old year, and baptise the new with libations of brandy or ale.

Windfall for a Fieldfare

C. HENRY WARREN

From the late 1930s, until his death in 1966, C. Henry Warren lived at Finchingfield, which he called Larkfield in his books, Happy Countryman, England is a Village, Adam was a Ploughman, The Scythe in the Apple Tree *and* Content With What I Have. *These books give an authentic picture of rural life during the 1940s and 1950s, except the first which relates to an earlier period.*

Had the incident occurred at any other time I should probably have thought it rather odd and left it at that. But coming as it did, on Christmas Eve, when one's mood is more

irrational than usual, more expectant, I must own it left a more insistent impression upon me.

Of course I might have remembered how, according to legend, the creature world should also be numbered among those who adored at the manger. Did not Piero della Franscesca, in his painting of the Nativity, add the braying of the ass to the chorus of carolling angels? And even Thomas Hardy, a sceptic if ever there was one, admitted in one of his best-known poems that he would willingly have left his Christmas hearth to go and see if the oxen were on their knees – 'hoping it might be so'.

If the ox and the ass are to be included in the festival, why not the birds also? Even that most unassuming of all our smaller English birds, the Hedge Sparrow (which isn't a sparrow at all, by the way), or dunnock, as it is more usually called? Anyway, it was a dunnock that set me off thinking about these things. If I could not go so far as to suggest it was actually adoring, I would have to own that it was certainly behaving in a fashion strangely becoming to the occasion.

I ought to explain that a pair of dunnocks had been much in evidence among the bird population of my garden all through the year. Not that there was anything unusual about this. Dunnocks are common enough in gardens, and their busy, not to say fussy, ground-keeping ways make them particularly obvious. It is not surprising that Essex people know them best by the endearing name of Hedge Betties. And so every day I would see the dumpy little creatures, quietly intent upon their business, usually not too far away from the hedge bottoms, where they nest, and where, after their manner, they could scurry away under the leaves at the least suggestion of danger.

If to be always following one another about, just a pace or two away from each other, is a sign of devotion, these were surely the most devoted bird-couple imaginable. They might

almost have been attached to one another by bits of invisible string. And when, as of course duly happened, the female bird retired to her nest to hatch out a family, the male bird looked quite lost, wandering about on his own. It is never a dunnock's way to keep a straight course as it goes foraging over the ground; but this one darted about so erratically that he almost seemed to be distrait, as if, deprived of his other self, he was no longer able to concentrate, no longer even quite sure what he was up to. All of which is nonsense, of course, but at any rate that was how he looked.

Happily, this business of bringing up a family ended at last. When the fledglings were able to fend for themselves, they went off (or, to be precise, they were driven off by their parents) to find a territory of their own to forage in; and so

Writtle Pond, Janaury 1987

the devoted couple were once more free to potter about the garden together, twittering occasionally to one another, giving little quick flicks of the wings, and generally keeping themselves to themselves as good dunnocks should.

Needless to say, after seeing so much of them over so long a period, I grew rather fond of them – if 'fond' is a permissible word to use of such a very one-sided relationship.

At least, I thought it was one-sided at the time; but after this Christmas Eve affair, I began to wonder if it were quite so one-sided after all. Perhaps the dunnocks were more grateful for the protective hospitality which my garden afforded than I had supposed at the time. Anyway, it would be nice to think so, however unornithological such a view might be.

I had been down to the village. In the crisp afternoon air, the place had the look of a Bewick engraving, one of his sharply bitten country winter tail-pieces. Children, muffled up to the chin, chased one another across the Green to keep warm, shouting and calling as they did so. Hooded women hurried to make their last-minute purchases at the little general stores, the tinkling of the door-bell providing a suitable accompaniment to their seasonable greetings. In fact, it seemed that every other word this afternoon was a greeting, and a warm, country-hearted one at that. However it might be elsewhere in the big, bickering world, here, in this tiny, remote corner of it, the good-will was true and warming.

And in the leafless lane, as I came home, it was greetings again, this time from the men coming off the fields. Cold as it was, with a pink-flushed sky betokening yet keener frost, I was warm at heart. I wanted to sing, and only deadening convention, which even this festive mood could not quite break down, prevented me from doing so.

The garden gate clicked to behind me. Coming up the path, I noticed something moving on one of the porch-posts, small and quiet as a mouse, and of much the same colour.

Then I saw it was a bird. Must be a tree-creeper, I thought. But a more careful scrutiny disclosed that it was a dunnock – one of my garden couple, no doubt. But it was alone, as the dunnocks never were. And anyway what was this one doing, climbing half-way up the porch?

I stayed where I was for a while, not daring to venture any nearer lest I should disturb the bird. With its tail glued down to the wood, and its buff-streaked back pricked out boldly in the low sunlight, it did not seem to be doing anything in particular, just clinging there. And since it did not fly away, or even stir much, I tip-toed nearer, step by slow step, until I was not more than a yard or so away. It only turned its head slightly to one side, looking back at me over its shoulder, hanging on to the post like a kitten that has climbed too far up a tree and does not know how to get down again. Its eyes were bright in their kohl-dark rims. It still made no attempt to fly away. And there we both stayed, each, it seemed, with something to say to the other, and yet no way of saying it.

I drew even closer, so close, indeed, that I could have put out my hand to the dunnock and taken it, which, presently, is exactly what I did. The wings fluttered a very little as I closed my fingers over them, but that was all: the bird remained otherwise quite passive, even as if it were used to this sort of thing every day. And the dusky eyes continued to look at me.

I wondered if perhaps it was injured in some way, so I examined it carefully, but I could find nothing amiss. I was mystified. That this ground-keeping, leaf-hiding bird should forsake its usual haunts and climb up my door was strange enough; but stranger was the fact that it should allow me to take it in my hand, in this unresisting way, and hold it, eye to eye.

Then suddenly I remembered what in the excitement of the moment I had forgotten: this was Christmas Eve. I smiled at the implied association and involuntarily stroked the soft down of the dunnock's head. Could some tragedy have

overtaken its mate? I reached out my free hand to open the door and take the bird into the house. But at that moment common sense intervened. A bird, so my saner self whispered to me, must take its chance like any other wild thing. Even in winter. Even when, perhaps, it has lost its mate. No good would come in the end from coddling it in an alien environment; it never does, as I have seen again and again.

So I carried the meek little dunnock over to the hedge and set it down, alone, among the tangled undergrowth where it belonged. Foolishly or not, however, a sense of guilt continued to haunt me for the remainder of the day; and even in the waking night I seemed to see those other-creature eyes looking into mine.

Christmas Eve – and once again there had been no room at the inn.

Christmas Pudding

S.L. BENSUSAN

Ephraim the carrier was a preacher in an Essex religious society known as the Peculiar People. Their divine service on Sunday was continuous until sunset and those attending took their meals with them.

'I never fare to see a Christmas puddin',' remarked Ephraim the Carrier solemnly, 'without I think o' me black Chris'mas what turned white by merracle.'

'I never heerd on't,' said the Man from Little Mudford, who constituted the audience.

'I hadn't acquainted along o' you then,' explained the Carrier. 'Did, you would have.'

'That ain't too late,' suggested the Man.

'Bein' there's nobody here,' agreed Ephraim. 'Most everybody else heerd it.' He poured his tea into the saucer and supped audibly.

'It's like this here,' he began. 'That was in th' year I bin an' lost me wife an' I doloured sore, f'r it was her habit to open th' door time I was out, an' to take me orders an' write 'em on a slate an' there must ha' bin a many what knocked an' got no answer an' went away an' sought somebody else.

'An' when Chris'mas was a comin', I should ha' said to some o' th' Brethren that I would fare to eat rough bein' there was nobody to cook f'r me. An' old Mrs Mace what was of th' Brethren and is now in glory, up an sez that she would make me a meat puddin' an' also a apple pasty an' likewise a Chris'mas puddin' an' that'd be three shillin's altogether. So I thanked her kindly an' give her th' money.'

'But that don't all goo as we expect in this here world,' continued Ephraim mournfully, 'an' come th' twenty-thard o' December, Mrs Mace's gran'son brought th' pasty an' th' ingredients f'r th' puddin', an' towd me as how Mrs Mace lay on her bed o' sickness an' could in no wise finish th' business, but if I liked, his mother, what was same as Mrs Mace's darter-in-law, 'd come in an' make th' puddin' on th' morrer. An' I no more to do but towd him to thank her kindly an' say I could manage. For that woman set under Reverend Spiller, what burnt incense an' encouraged 'bominations an' believed in Transubstation, that false an' pornicious doctrine, an' would ha' bowed down to th' Pope if so be he'd come to Maychester, an' would ha' fallen down before him an' likewise worshipped him.'

Exhausted by the effort, Ephraim paused and poured out more tea while the Man looked on with admiration.

'Now,' continued the Carrier after recovering breath, 'I set down an' mixed all them ingrediments like I'd seen me wife do many's th' time, an' I broke a egg over 'em an' likewise stirred 'em, an' tied 'em up in a bit o' rag an' set 'em in a saucepan on th' fire to bile.'

'An' nex' day, time I come in, a little afore Chris'mas Eve, I took out th' puddin' from th' saucepan an' took th' rag off. An' that puddin' fell all over th' dish like it worn't a puddin' at all, an' I set down by me fire an' doloured more'n ever because o' me wife what I'd lost. For she made puddin's that was masters, every etch one on 'em.'

'Then,' continued Ephraim slowly and solemnly, 'I fared to rebuke meself an' I sez to meself that I was a back-slider an' dedn't have no faith. An' I recalled how them ravens bin an' fed th' Prophet Elijah, an' I sez to meself that what a man needs is not puddin' so much as belief. Now I had not set there an hour, first a dolourin' an' then a comfortin' o' meself, when come a tap at th' door an' Miss Arabella, th' Squire's sister, come in. An' I see a puddin' basin in her hand.'

'"Good arternoon, Efrum," she sez, an' I up an' welcomed her gladly.'

'"Miss Arabella," I sez, "I was expectin' of a raven an' now you bin' an' come." An' she seemed reg'lar vexed.'

'"I ain't no raven, Efrum," she sez, "an' I'm surprised at you bein' so rude."'

'Then I up an' sez, "Miss Arabella, do not be surprised, ne yet distarbed, ne yet disquieted, but when you bin an' finished your errand o' marcy an' left me that there puddin', read Kings One, Chapter Seventeen. But afore you do that, do you be so kind as to come an' explain an' likewise larn me, why this here puddin' o' mine, what I have truly an' faithfully

biled, bin an' fell down same as them walls o' Jericho fell, time Joshua blew agin 'em"'

By now the Carrier was talking in his full pulpit tones, those he uses when addressing the Peculiar People. He continued mournfully:

'Miss Arabella see I was right, an' she come forward an' 'xamined the Chris'mas puddin' what I made, an' she sez, "Efrum, that ain't bound itself 'cause you bin an' forgot th' suet."'

'Then I up an' sez, "Ma'am, you have bin an' saved me from th' oppressor," an' she should say, "she was reg'lar glad," an' went her way, an' come Chris'mas Day I fared wunnerful.'

'That was a odd accident to my thinkin',' said the Man from Mudford.

'No, me friend,' declared the Carrier, 'that worn't no accident, that was same as a plot, to undo me an' to vex me an' likewise to upset me.'

'Mrs Mace's darter-in-law must ha' left out th' suet a pu'pose like, time she sent me them ingrediments. An' I do not doubt but that Reverend Spiller ordered her to do it, bein' full o' hatred agin me because I will not bow down to th' Pope ne yet worship him. But he has not pervaled agin me arter all, f'r he is dead an' gone, an' I'm a eatin' Chris'mas puddin' even to this day.'

At Coggeshall

REVEREND DAVID BEETON

The Reverend David Beeton has been Vicar of St Peter ad
Vincula, Coggeshall, since 1981. He was ordained in 1965
and served as curate in the parish of St Edmund, King and
Martyr, Forest Gate, before becoming Vicar of St Augustine of
Canterbury, Rush Green, Romford in 1971.
The parish church of Coggeshall was bombed during the war
and extremely well restored in 1956. The church is open every
day and visitors are welcome.

In Coggeshall – lying on the A120, a mile or so north of the great A12 – the town lights and tree go up the week after Remembrance Sunday. This is usually followed by a reminder, from one of the antique dealers of Coggeshall, to the vicar, that Christmas is coming and 'shouldn't the stars be shining on the Church?' Some years ago now, after having the lights on the Christmas tree in the churchyard vandalized, the Tower Captain made a star for the south face of the church tower which is vandal proof. The antique dealer loved it so much that he paid for the others to be made so that whichever way you approach Coggeshall a star on the church tower will remind you of the famous Star of Bethlehem which led the wise men to the Christ child. Every year, with the reminder, he offers a donation to cover the additional cost of the electricity and bulbs. The reason for the reminder is not the forgetfulness of the vicar, nor the Tower Captain and his wife, who have to fix the stars, but the fact that we who worship in

Coggeshall parish church

the church refuse to begin the Christmas countdown until the ancient season of Advent begins four Sundays before Christmas.

Like most churches we have an Advent wreath, with its evergreen cut from the churchyard, and its four candles to be lit in increasing numbers as the Sundays of Advent come along until all four burn on the last Sunday proclaiming the coming of the Saviour – the Light of the World. This stands on a circular table on the chancel step between the choir

stalls, but at Christmas it is moved to a position by the pulpit and an additional candle is placed in the centre to represent the Christ Child. Last year gilded twigs were added and all sorts of carved wooden ornaments hung upon them representing the many different facets of our lives, with the Light of the World shining on them and through them all.

Advent Sunday has the normal pattern of our Sunday worship but a special United Service is held in the evening with Readings and Carols proclaiming the truths of the Christian faith.

So Advent takes its course – joyful and expectant. Just as we hold back to the beginning of Advent – so we hold back at the end of Advent. No Christmas carols until Christmas Eve; and no decorations until after morning service of the fourth Sunday in Advent. A twenty-five foot tree may well be in place; but not a single decoration is on it. But after the service it is full steam ahead to decorate the tree; arrange the crib with its figures of the Virgin and St Joseph, the shepherds and the angel; decorate the pillars – all twelve of them – with garlands and candles, stars or angels; and the rest of the church with holly and ivy and other decorations. We do try hard to decorate the church and arrange the crib in a different style and manner each year. Many people are bustling around doing all this to ensure, as John Betjeman declares in his Christmas poem, 'the Church looks nice on Christmas Day'. Really we want more than that; we want the church building to proclaim the truth that the Saviour of the World has been born for us – and we are grateful.

Coggeshall is a fairly small market town and we have an extremely good relationship between the different denominations. Consequently, we all join together at Christ Church on the fourth Sunday in Advent, in the evening, for a carol service, but Christmas really starts in the parish church at six o'clock on Christmas Eve when we have a family carol

St Peter ad Vincula, Coggeshall. This large fifteenth-century church
is one hundred and twenty feet long

service followed by a great exodus experience as we all walk
down to the Market Square and sing carols by the town tree.
The midnight mass fills our large parish church of St Peter ad
Vincula and the bells ring out the Good News, and the tiny
figure of the Christ child is placed in the manger of the crib.
Christmas is here. Happy Christmas everybody. It only
remains for us to try and proclaim the same Good News and
Love every day in our lives.

Even three services on Christmas morning, including one at our beloved St Nicholas Chapel – the former Gatehouse Chapel of the abbey built in 1120 – do not bring us to the end of our public celebrations for the birth of the Lord Jesus. For many years now we have provided a lunch for any who are alone at Christmas or housebound. They can come to the church hall or vicarage and eat and drink together, transport provided of course, or they can have meals delivered to their homes. There is tremendous co-operation in providing and preparing the turkey, sausages, stuffing, bread sauce, cranberry sauce, potatoes, parsnips, carrots and gravy, Christmas pudding, mince pies and brandy cream sauce as well as hostess trollies, and everyone, including the helpers, sits down to an excellent meal.

Weary, but not totally beaten, many stroll along to the parish church at four o'clock for a story and carols round the crib; the Saviour of the World has indeed been born and lives again through all our lives. Then it's a cup of tea and Christmas cake before going back to our own homes.

We are very fortunate in Coggeshall in having a number of ancient charities which are able to provide the housebound and elderly (over eighty years) with gifts of money and chocolates each Christmas and Easter. From Boxing Day onwards the housebound and elderly know the truth of the final couplet of John Betjeman's poem:

> That God was man in Palestine
> And lives today in Bread and Wine

as the Blessed Sacrament is taken to them in their homes.

We are grateful for Christmas in Coggeshall, and hope that in our town, each day can, in a sense, be a Christmas Day, filled with the love of God incarnate for all mankind.

Bring in the Holly

C. HENRY WARREN

This extract is taken from The Scythe in the Apple Tree, *published in 1953. The author had been living in a thatched cottage called Timbers just outside Finchingfield for the last sixteen years.*

It was Christmas Eve, and during the afternoon I went to see my friends at Thurstons Farm. A milky fog hid the countryside, where the only sound was of small water-drops dripping from hedge and tree. Everything was unnaturally still – attentive, or so it seemed, to something not yet audible to the human ear.

I had not met a soul all the way; and then, just as I was nearing the farm, suddenly, as if from nowhere, Dave Johnson appeared, followed by his three goats. With his hands stuck in his trousers pockets, leaving the long wrists showing bare, and his jacket collar pulled up round his chin, Dave walked slowly, silently, along the grass verge; and his goats stepped daintily beside him, shaking the peeled sticks which he has slung round their necks to prevent them (only they do not) from straying into people's yards and gardens.

'A merry Christmas!' Dave shouted and at once disappeared, goats and all, like a desert shepherd passing in the mists.

There was silence again, heavy and wet and lonely.

And then it was old Ernie who appeared, just as

mysteriously, his smiling face framed in the fog as he peered over the garden hedge. Soon he was joined by his wife, neat and trim as ever.

'A merry Christmas to you, sir!' she said, for she has an old-fashioned courtesy, a gentility, rare in the countryside these days. And then, holding out a small paper parcel, she added: 'If you are going round to the farm, I wonder if you would mind taking this to the lady?'

At the farm itself the same wish greeted me through the open kitchen door. Mrs Jackson was busy over the stove, cooking the Christmas delicacies, and Eddie was washing his weekly collection of ducks' eggs in the sink, ready for the eggman (as he is called) to take to the Packing Station. It was the sign of their friendly acceptance of me that they did not for a moment pause in their tasks. I shook the drops from my coat and sat down.

Outside the windows nothing was visible except the grey dusk of the fog; but a farm-house kitchen declares itself for what it is without the aid of a view over barn and byre, field and corn stack. It is the focus of the life of the farmstead; always there is some activity; always there is somebody coming or going. For fruitful friendliness I would choose Thurstons kitchen above any other I know. And so it was now. The spirit could not help blossoming in such a place – and perhaps especially on Christmas Eve.

Presently the farmer himself came in, the faithful spaniel at his heels. His eyebrows glistened with fog, his boots were covered with mud, there was the smell of cattle in his clothes.

'A merry Christmas!' he said, and well enough one could hear that he meant it to the full.

A merry Christmas – it is the word they all use here, the unashamed old greeting of the season which Englishmen have spoken through the centuries until lack of faith and excess of commercial enterprise have at last rendered it all but

meaningless. But it is not meaningless to these people living miles from anywhere, remote from any centre but that of their own quiet, fertile lives. Merry they say and merry they mean: never mind what greeting others may use to-day.

. . . I made my way home at length, loaded with the gifts that had accompanied the simple wishes. The fog was clearing a little now and the true twilight descending. I came past an occasional cottage, with its paper decorations gaudy in the naked lamplight; past a week-ender's house, with its discreet crimson shades over the candles on the tea-table; past old George, shuffling along the lane, pushing a pile of Christmas wood on his rickety trolley. I set the presents on the table. A bottle of home-made mead; some Bramley apples, newly taken from a clamp in the garden, crisp and firm as the day they were picked; a pat of Jersey butter and a jam jar of cream; a sackful of holly in berry. What essential country

The Pond, Theydon Bois

presents they were, seeming to give so much more than themselves! And how eloquently they spoke of their givers – old Ernie and Dave, Mrs Jackson and the rest!

Under the ivy-twined beams that night and the bright red berries shining in the lamplight, I sat before the fire, when everybody else had gone to bed, listening to a recorded broadcast of the afternoon Carol Service from King's Chapel, Cambridge.

Double creatures that we are, pagan and Christian at one and the same time! We hang up the holly and the ivy, the yew and the mistletoe, in token, although we no longer acknowledge it, of the woodland gods, the woodland spirits, that ask to be taken indoors for a respite from the winter weather, to repay us for our kindness, who knows how, through the years to come. And then, sitting under their green shine, we join with heart, if not, these days, with voice, in the old carols that tell of a child who from His bed in the meagre straw smiled on the dark world He had come to lighten with His love.

Listening to the pure-toned voices of the boys as they sang those simple tunes of Christmas and to the experienced voices, full of character, of the men as they read the story of that long-ago birthday in Bethlehem, I thanked the inventors who had made it possible for me thus to span the miles and to bring back lost time at the mere twisting of a knob.

While I had been on my way up to the farm in the foggy afternoon, and Dave had gone by with his train of goats, and old Ernie's gentle wife had leaned over the hedge to ask me to take her Christmas gift to 'the lady', this Carol Service had been echoing under the vaulted roof of King's Chapel, where the still candle-flames shone on the age-black oak, and the Tudor roses blossomed enduringly in stone; but science had found the trick of capturing the winged sounds, and passed it on to me, so that I might loosen them on the air again to-night, here in the quiet room.

When the last Amen had died away and in the midnight silence I could hear only the small cracklings of the burning wood on the hearth, I sat on awhile in the still house thinking over the words I had been listening to. From the mantelpiece I took down the Christmas poem a friend had sent me:

> . . . Yes! And this is your house we cheer,
> Cheer this singular night;
> Our breath smokes well upon midnight air;
> Look out of window and find our light;
> Only a stable lantern still,
> Lit by a candle small and clear;
> And we sing, Peace, to men of goodwill.
> Does any such man live here?

I opened the window and leaned out into the solemn, breathing darkness. From down in the village, carried to me on the thick, wet air, came the pealing of the church bells. 'A merry Christmas,' I said in my heart, 'and Peace, to men of goodwill!'

Poet's Christmas

ALFRED TENNYSON

While living at High Beech, Tennyson wrote to a friend, 'I
have been at this place in Epping Forest all the year, with
nothing but that muddy pond in prospect.' But when the pond
was frozen he used to skate on it, wearing a long blue cloak.

At Francis Allen's on the Christmas-eve, –
The game of forfeits done – the girls all kiss'd
Beneath the sacred bush and past away –
The parson Holmes, and poet Everard Hall,
The host, and I sat round the wassail-bowl,
Then half-way ebb'd: and there we held a talk,
How all the old honour had from Christmas gone,
Or gone, or dwindled down to some odd games
In some old nooks like this; till I, tired out
With cutting eights that day upon the pond,
Where, three times slipping from the outer edge,
I bump'd the ice into three several stars,
Fell in a doze.

Arise, Sir Loin!

ANON.

A snowstorm once interrupted Charles II's hunting in Epping
Forest and his party went to Pimp Hall for shelter according to
an old ballad where there was a loin of beef upon the table.
Another story places the incident at Copt Hall while other
stories attribute the 'Knighting' to James I and Henry VIII.

The Second Charles of England
Rode forth one Christmastide
To hunt a gallant stag of ten,
Of Chingford woods the pride.

Quoth Charles: Odds fish! a noble dish,
And noble made by me,
By kingly rite, I dub thee knight –
Sir Loin henceforward be.

Carol Singing

SPIKE MAYS

Spike Mays was born in 1907 at a hamlet near the village of Asdon in north-west Essex. In 1969 his book Reuben's Corner *was published, from which the following extract is taken; a sequel,* Return to Anglia, *appeared in 1986. Both books are, as* The Times Literary Supplement *said, a continuous cascade of anecdotes.*

At Christmas it was a different matter. Most of the choir, and sometimes Bartlow Hamlet only, would band together for carol singing. We would walk miles and miles through the deepest drifts, to all the Ends, singing louder and longer than we ever did at church.

For this we made our own lanterns – jam jars with candles, of which we each had one. Usually a dozen or more of us would set out, all jam-jarred and collector-boxed. Muffs, helmets, scarves, winter-warmers and leggings made from old sacks were the garments we wore to keep out the cold. People could see us for miles before they heard us for our lights were easily discerned in a largely lightless land. It must have looked a pretty straggling torchlight procession from the distant view but close up we no doubt looked much better and more Christmasy – all red of cheek, our frosty breath blowing into the air pinked and yellowed by the candlelight. Farmers were the best payers – Tilbrooks, Furzes, Haggers and Webbs. Usually they would invite us in, particularly if they had been at the bottle, to sing to them in the warm, and

we would then get silver instead of copper plus mince pies and lovely yellow apples, the latter all mellow and brown-pippy through ripening on oat straw in lofts. Now and again they would give us wine and small beer. The wine was all right because it warmed us up but the small beer made our teeth chatter and our voices quiver.

Sometimes we used to cheat a bit by not singing the proper words.

> Beer by the pailful, makes us gay, triumphant,
> Bring some, ye citizens of Steventon's End.
> Fetch out the mince pies, hot and sweet and ta-sty;
> If you don't we'll bash your door in;
> We'll bash your silly door in;
> We'll bash your silly door in,
> As sure as we're born.

We only sang such words to those who were too mean to open the door. If we sang one word wrong inside a house the news would go round the village and the parson would tick us off for not doing the job properly.

Old Johnny Purkis came with us one night. He couldn't sing a bit, nor could he do the church job he had as well as it should have been done. Johnny was the organ blower. Many a time he let Mabel Eason down by not pumping when wind was required. He would sit in a little recess at the back of the organ all by himself, screened from the congregation by green curtains. Mabel would know the moment he arrived, for he would swish the curtains close with a great flourish, making the brass rings dance and jingle on their rail. From that moment she had to hope for the best. Sometimes he would drop off to sleep and the organ would groan and splutter to a stop in the middle of a hymn or psalm. Sometimes he would snore, or make the loudest of rude noises and the

The choir at St Mary's church, Saffron Walden, singing outside the
West Door, 1960

churchwarden would nip smartly round to tell him off and
ginger him up.

We took him carol singing because he was the best man in
Essex for walking straight in snow and could lead the way.
This was curious because when roads were clear he would
lurch from side to side – as though completely without
control of his spindly legs. In this day and age old Johnny
would not have lasted ten seconds.

Between Christmas and the New Year there was always a
spate of choral and bell-ringing practice. On one occasion the
Reverend Hartley had got a bit frosty over something or other
and had doubled practice nights to two per week. Rumour
had it that Starchy Williams had complained and advised that
we choirboys should be gingered up. With that end in view

we were ordered to report to the parish church where the campanologists were ringing out wild bells to the wild sky – instead of to the Sunday school building. There was plenty of flying cloud and several degrees of frost on that wintry night – enough to crisp the top of a thick blanket of snow.

Poddy Coote, the leading choir boy, thereupon hatched a plot. When everybody else was wending their way to home and fireside, there was one who was not. Lo and behold, it was Starchy. By some unaccountable circumstance he found himself alone . . . locked in the belfry.

And when all the Christian folk of Ashdon had gone upstairs; were on their knees a-saying prayers – including the Reverend Hartley – a sound rang through the wintry night. One wild bell alone was ringing to the wild sky. It was not the customary steady toll, more of a feverish clanging.

When the Reverend Hartley arrived at the church, after plodding through half a mile of deep snow drifts, to let Starchy loose, he had to make the same trip all over again – twice. He had forgotten the key.

'Retribushun!' said the leading choir boy. 'That's what it were, retribushun!'

He may have been right. Anyway, the choir practices were halved forthwith.

Midnight Mass

ETHELIND FEARON

This is a further extract from Most Happy Husbandman.
Ethelind Fearon also wrote Me and Mr Mountjoy *(Mr
Mountjoy was a female pig),* The Making of a Garden*,* The
Reluctant Gardener*, and* The Reluctant Cook.

Of all the lovely services in the length of the year, the
midnight mass on Christmas Eve has always been the best. A
most acceptable and pleasant feast of light and sound, and a
worshipping in excelsis of all they stand for. Indeed, to see the
ecstasy of devotion with which the village, and in fact the
Wise Men from very far afield, gather round the crib, arouses
at times a feeling of slight misgiving. Are we, then, heathen,
that we bow down to gods of wood and stone? Are we pagans,
that we hold such high revelry at midnight on Christmas Eve?

But all the robes and banners, the fugues and candles and
wreathed incense clouds, are but the outward expression of an
inward spiritual necessity, to worship beauty in whatever form
it comes. And since all the light and sound and colour are but
symbols of Him who said 'Let there be Light', we are in fact
adoring the Lord God who made them all.

And within, it is all light. Light and bright and high. So
wide and high that in it a man may stand up, take breath, and
let his soul expand. And of such infinite variety that one
might for ever study it, and forever discover some new thing.

Since the day when no light might gleam into the
darkness, no bell open its throat and sing, we have had no

midnight mass. But this year, none but those who achieved the miracle knows how or why, we have been allowed to gather again at the old time. Briefly, and dimly, it is true, but all the faithful flocked to attend it with joy and thanksgiving.

I had thought that nothing could strike deeper into one's æsthetic consciousness than our service of other years. Then, candles winked and glowed from every corner. Candles in the stella swung high within the chancel arches. Candles on the high Christmas trees between every pair of massive pillars in the nave. Candles round the crib, candles before the Virgin, before St Joan, in the Becket Chapel, the Lady Chapel; every little shrine everywhere was a glowing pool of light in the scented dusk. One was lapped about softly by outer darkness, in which a hypnotic galaxy of stars imprisoned in the delicate windows, winked like black diamonds from on high.

This year we had three shrouded candles. One to the north, one to the south, and one far far away on the High Altar. And it was magnificent. A service in silhouette, in which long, two-dimensional shadows came and went, and mysteriously cast another shadow, faint, like the reflection of a rainbow.

One was dismembered, non-corporeal, alone with God, and if one had a neighbour, neither felt his presence, nor knew whom he might be.

Forms without faces slid to and fro, chanted, and sang unaccompanied softly up to heaven, and the notes dripped back again from the high roof, gently, like warm rain. The brave pennants that by day flaunt their purple and peach and gold from the clerestory hung black and lifeless, giant bats with folded wings, asleep under the carven cobwebbed monsters glowering from the roof.

And the one small candle by the altar's cross achieved a significance that was not only decorative and symbolic but geographical. It was a point to march on as we went to receive the host. A star shining from the darkness to guide our feet,

Matching

lest the unwary traveller strayed into the trackless wastes that beset him on either side, and never could return.

It was a service of ghosts in a ghostly world, and outside were the darkness, the stars, and silence.

But on Christmas morning all was brave with colour and golden robes. We put on again our former trappings and rejoiced to our hearts content. Bells, silent since their purpose was restricted to one of urgent warning, and not of happy summons, let loose their tongues upon the morning air, and tossed their ton-weight heads in joyful liberation. 'Christus natus' they sang, and beneath them we sang too.

If the orchestra had been unable to play the night before, because they couldn't read their music, they made up for it now. The oboe and the 'cello are professionals, but this time they play for love alone, and the rest of the orchestra, recruited solely from the village, are so good that they are a pleasure to the ear. The padre, continuing a musical tradition that began when Wydow was vicar in 1481, has a wonderful way with his raw material. He puts an instrument into its hand, says, 'Make a noise, *some* noise, *any* noise, so long as it *is* a noise. And then, presently, you will be able to make the *right* noise.'

And presently, miraculously, it is so. By being alternately patient, brutal, diplomatic, stern, tone-deaf or stone-deaf, as the occasion demands, he has taught them all to play the right notes at the right time, and the result is ravishing. They are school children, school teachers, land girls, farmers, people with lots of money and no jobs, people with nothing much of anything but spare time, and representatives of practically every trade in the village, fiddling, fluting, drumming and horning like archangels.

And the choir? Well, they have had the loving hand of several masters to form and guide them, beginning with Holst himself, and I can only say that I believe even he would

feel they had done well this day. Attack and rhythm are utterly beyond reproach, and the quality of their tone like mole-skin stroked the wrong way, velvety, with that extra bit of crispness which makes all the difference.

The procession is forming as the organ softly wanders through *I saw Three Ships*. There is a bobbing about of choir boy's candles until they get settled into place, a tall one with the heavy cross and the infantile cherubs with swinging lanterns and censer. Banners of the Virgin and St George, the singer's banner, the Jerusalem banner, and the rest, gather into place, each tasselled and ribboned, with children in bright headdresses to hold the ribbons. Between the last two banners walks the congregation.

How they all arrived will always be a mystery.

Transport was always difficult, and now that it is impossible, the perversity of man decrees that the whole world shall come. By 'bus from Cambridge, Colchester, Chelmsford; by train, walking, bicycling, or merely staying with relations, nevertheless they come, in the most astonishing numbers. There are half a dozen different uniforms, three Poles, a Czech, Americans, Canadians, and a dark West Indian. People of all denominations and most professions, authors, artists, film stars, two MPs, a woman sculptor, a wood carver, a composer, and people with wide black felts, ambitions, and no professional status at all. And the village is here en masse. I imagine that every turkey in the place has been left roasting alone, while its owners salve their souls with music and rejoicing.

The huge winding procession is now moving, pacing slowly the long aisles as the choir sing with throbbing ardour 'adeste fideles', and waves of lovely sound come and go, as one nears or retreats from the orchestra. The vicar is towards the front, all glorious in brocade and golden trappings, curates behind him, not noticeably less well arrayed, and a phalanx of

choir boys in scarlet and lace, and choir girls in chiffon head veils, dripping their rainbow cascades to the floor.

In and out we go, past the lectern, the Chapel of St Catherine, and the Becket Chapel, 'God of God, Light of Light,' we chant, 'O come let us adore Him'.

Adore is a lovely word to sing, a comfortable vowel to hold roundly in the mouth.

Past the Chapel of Our Lady and Our Lady Annie now, winding by the sacristy and the shrine of Blessed Thomas More. The fringe of the last banner waves forward, every now

North Porch, St John the Baptist church, Thaxted. The church is one hundred and eighty-three feet long, the spire one hundred and eight feet high. In the fourteenth and fifteenth centuries Thaxted was one of the most prosperous towns in Essex

99

and then, tickling the back of my neck like a gently nuzzling mouse.

Up past the children's altar, belfry and font. 'Sing choirs of angels, sing in exultation.' The choir is magnificently doing just this, with a fine fervour, while we return down the nave, stand for a Hail Mary, and then prop banners against pillars, place the candles on the floor, and slide back to our seats again.

The service wends its solemn way through prayers, chants, and Latin responses. In this, as in most other things we remain doggedly, almost savagely, unchanged, and it is that lovely order of the first English Mass of 1549 to which we cling today. The priest, standing in a shaft of morning sunlight far away under the east window, chants a stave, and the choir take it up, repeat it, wind it into a delicate arabesque, and gently let it fall again.

Lovely phrase piles on lovely phrase. 'Blessed passion, mighty resurrection and glorious ascension – unworthy through our manifold sins – bounden duty and service', and then we are completely encompassed in silence as he prays alone on the green carpeted steps, a silence built not of solitude, but from a common worship of a common God, a unity of thought and purpose.

That particular moment of time seems to hang suspended in eternity like a golden ball, almost one can feel the descent of the Holy Ghost.

And then the ball is shattered, as a little bell shrills, and up and up, to the angels guarding the roof, rises a choir boy's golden voice in a delicately winding Amen, and into the pool of quiet drop pearls of perfect sound. 'Agnus Dei' they sing, 'O Lamb of God, that takest away the sins of the world'.

The congregation walk softly up to the altar, relay after relay, while the choir by the west door sing, in broad sweep of subtly woven sound, gently, and unaccompanied, a Holst

Hosanna, and a morsel of William Byrd who lived and died near to this place, and then we sit back and relax a little before the offertory. I replace the good serviceable half-crown that lay nestling under my hand, and fumble for something more adequate, and Sally joins sweetly in the carol *Away in a Manger*, as the plates go round.

Presently the choir is being whipped crisply through the hoops by some unseen but galvanic baton, behind a huge pillar. Probably Imogen, I think, it sounds like her dynamic touch, and then, in their turn, the orchestra, under the same superb handling, have slid into something strange and lovely. A fragile, iridescent fragment that might be Benjamin Britten, but is difficult to ascribe to any hand or era.

'That's funny,' murmurs a man behind me, 'the notes are different.'

But they're not, of course, they never were. It's the intervals that make the difference, not the notes. And it crosses my mind that perhaps it's that way with everything, the intangible that counts. It's the shadows within an elm that make it a thing to wonder at, and the spaces in a design that make the lines worth while.

The priest is now pronouncing the Benediction, and we sit for our final feast. The orchestra, just a shade too pianissimo, begins Bach's *Little Fugue*, which, before we've finished with it, will fill the church with waves of rolling sound, and evoke from my neighbour the complaint that it's blasting the ears off him.

The wood-wind are chasing each other upstairs and downstairs all over the place, with the oboe leading, tonguing it with a pretty combination of spit and whistle. Skip, pirouette, wriggle, goes the tune, and, as children will, his little brothers the flutes and clarinets copy the oboe, a shade higher up the scale. The bassoon and double bass see the joke, and gurgle like mad while the rest of the orchestra join in a

lovely contrapuntal giggle down in the bass, the woodcutter on a Boehm flute having a meaty little piece all to himself, and a farmer putting in some good work on a viola.

I can just see Helga farther down the aisle, and she appears to be blanketed in a layer of impassivity you could cut with a knife, but her eyes are shining.

We are nearly through when I feel a little hand creeping into mine, and look down to see how Sally fares. It's rather heady stuff, and she's apt to take these things to heart. Only the other day she told me that Handel's *Queen of Sheba* was her favourite tune, and when I asked why, said, 'because of the proud pattern it makes in my head'.

As she looks up at me now, her face is greenish-white, and her eyes like two burnt holes in a blanket. 'I big you pardin, Daddy,' she gulps, 'could you please make a scene for me to go behind, I'm going to be sick in a minnit.'

I seek a way of escape, but it is slow and too difficult. 'Hang on, honey,' I implore, 'in less than a minute it'll be over, and you won't feel so excited, but use my hat if you must.' And I return thanks that it is only my old stitched tweed hat, which I'd snatched in a hurry, and not my good felt.

But the danger is averted, the fugue finishes with a final terrific blast from everyone at once, and after a moment they slide into the innocuous and honey-sweet *O that we were there*, and we begin moving out. But not right out, that would be too sudden.

The priests depart to unrobe, and the congregation wander over to the crib, to stand over the warm gratings in the floor over the boiler-room and toss cheery inconsequential greetings over each other's heads.

Marian is waylaid by a large but well-girt female in horn-rims and hand-weaving. She bounces and beams – old college chum, obviously. Two people thank me for books which I

didn't send, and Tom Hoskyn forgets to mention the bottle of Scotch which I did. A small girl with a large doll and minute wood-like pigtails navigates two rows of chairs at a run, comes hopping up on one leg and says breathlessly, 'Hello, Mr Fearon, where's Sally, Happy Christmas, isn't the crib lovely, Joseph's got a patch on his elbow just like Daddy, I got this doll in my stocking, I want to show it to Sally, I know you but you don't know me, I'm Daddy's daughter, oh, there's Sally, good-bye.'

All very amiable and ambiguous.

My face is stiff with smiling and saying, 'And to you too.' I am thinking about the turkey, and I want a pipe.

And presently we move off, and the whole eight bells let themselves go again as if they were trying to make up for four years of silence in one terrific peal.

'Happy Christmas to you, Fred. Happy Christmas, George.'

'Same to you, sir, and many of 'em.'

Peace on earth among men of goodwill.

'God bless us every one.'

Siren Night and Silent Night

BRIAN MELLISH

Brian Mellish was born in 1940 at Dagenham. His house was in the last street of Metropolitan Essex. Beyond lay a huge cornfield and in the middle distance the wooded hills running up to Lambourne End could be seen: Hainault Forest, remnant of the vast Essex Forest of the Middle Ages. He now farms at Mautby in Norfolk.

The first Christmas I can remember is the one of 1944. My sister, Sheila, three years older than I, had with my help – if help if could be called – spent many evenings cutting strips of coloured paper which she had gathered from various sources. The strips of paper were then pasted together to form chains which were now festooned in the kitchen and sitting room. Paper bells, coloured balls, were hung about the pictures of Harlequin and Columbine which hung in our living room. Sprigs of holly – illegally obtained on our last visit to the Forest – were tucked behind the chiming clock and the pair of china dogs on the mantelshelf which were half-hidden by a number of Christmas cards.

Before teatime on Christmas Eve I accompanied Sheila on her visits to her friends when they exchanged small homemade gifts. Our last call was to June Nelson, a special friend of Sheila's, who lived opposite to us. As we left, she

followed us out into the street and pointed to the darkening sky. Looking eastwards, she said, 'Look for the moving star over Bethlehem.' We all looked, two seven year old girls and a four year old boy. We all saw the star.

That night, in the east, there were lights of a different kind. 'Go to sleep,' said Mother. 'It's only God's fireworks.' But Mother's tense body and the earlier sound of sirens told us that those 'fireworks' were an air raid, probably on nearby Hornchurch Airfield.

Despite the air raid, the excitement and anticipation of Christmas had tired us and we were soon asleep. In Mother's bed, as always on such nights when the siren wailed. I suppose she thought it better that we should all go or survive together.

We knew nothing until we awoke next morning. Not in Mother's bed but in the living room where there was already a blazing fire. Mother had carried us there during the raid and put us in a makeshift bed surrounded by a wire mesh frame supporting on its top a thick sheet of steel; our indoor air raid shelter.

At the foot of this bed and hanging on a hook that also held our gas masks there were, not stockings, but pillow cases, bulging, even though it was a time of austerity. Sheila and I gasped and fell on these cornucopias.

First there was a small mesh stocking containing an apple, an orange and some cobnuts. A colouring book with a picture of a lion on the cover. A little wooden man, fixed on a frame, which did all manner of gyrations and acrobatics when the string attached to his body was pulled. (This toy had been made by my grandfather.) Then a set of cardboard skittles; a magnificent grey battleship bristling with panel pin guns (made by George Wright, our neighbour next door, from offcuts of wood gleaned while repairing bomb damaged houses). Next came newly knitted gloves, hats and a pullover

in Fair Isle pattern. My sister had a china doll which she seemed to like and which to my mind made a noise more like a bleating sheep than a baby.

There were also skipping ropes, whipping tops, bouncing balls, sets of five stones and my first box of marbles. These last presents were very important in the lives of children. These simple pieces of equipment would keep us occupied in the backyard or in the street all the year round. I suppose we were the last generation of children to inherit the culture of street games which had been handed down for centuries. Skipping; either by one girl on her own or, with a long rope stretched across the street, with half-a-dozen boys and girls and this was always accompanied by a chant. Hopscotch was played by chalking squares on the pavement stones. Small groups played five stones or marbles, a girl alone would bounce a ball or juggle one, two or three balls in the air.

After we had opened our presents and dressed in front of the fire, the wireless was switched on and after it had warmed up it was tuned for us to hear the Christmas Bells.

We all had a letter from my father who was serving in the army in Algeria. My letter consisted of some drawings of aeroplanes and ships and a little note which had to be read to me. It took pride of place on the mantelshelf.

Christmas dinner; what a feast! Roast potatoes, parsnips, Brussels sprouts, and carrots all grown by Mother on her allotment, and rabbit stuffed with sage and onions. In the summer it was my sister's and my job to gather food for the rabbits; dandelions (which stained our hands), sow thistles, cow parsley and grass by the sackful. In the winter the rabbits had to make do with the trimmings of greens from the greengrocer, a little hay, and household scraps mixed with bran.

Our Christmas pudding was date pudding with a sprig of holly on the top.

Writtle, January 1987

After dinner we played with our new toys on the luxurious new peg mat. Mother had been working hard for several months making this mat, with Christmas as her deadline. It was no ordinary rag mat. Somehow she had managed to obtain some thick yarn which she then dyed into differen

colours before cutting up. We had all helped, especially with cutting it into small lengths ready for the ties. I had even used the special peg to push the yarn through the canvas backing and then to knot the yarn. No doubt my efforts had to be unpicked and re-done after I had gone to bed. To us, on this Christmas Day, our carpet which must have been at least three yards square, was as good as the best Wilton.

Our really special present, which was from Father, had yet to be opened; it had been saved for our afternoon delight. Mother removed the wrapping paper to uncover a box on which were pictured clusters of exotic fruits; apricots, figs. . . . She opened the box. A puff of blue smoke arose. Was this some magic from the mystic east? No, the crystalised fruits for which poor Father had saved his meagre allowance were just blue-green mouldy puff-balls.

'Never mind, let's have some lemonade and hazel nuts,' said Mother, 'they'll be just as nice.' But oh, how she would have liked to have tasted just one apricot. The slight quiver in the corner of Mother's mouth belied her cheerfulness. She was, no doubt, wondering how to break the news to Father and imagining his disappointment.

Tea was an effort, as Christmas tea always is, but trifle and iced Christmas cake could not be refused.

After tea the lights were turned off and the three of us sat round the fire and sang carols. Was Father, the father I could not remember, sitting round a fire in the desert singing carols? We liked to think so.

There were no sirens, no air raids; it was a quiet night.

A Doctor's Christmas, 1930

GEOFFREY BARBER

Dr Geoffrey Barber was in practice at Dunmow and High Easter from 1930 until his retirement in 1963. His book, Country Doctor, *was published in 1973.*

The prevalent illnesses differed in many ways from those which we meet today. Broadly, they were due to poverty and deficiency, whereas nowadays they are more likely to be caused by affluence and excess. The old people, and parents and children in large families, tended to be short of food, badly clothed, and poorly housed in damp old cottages with no drains. It was all very picturesque in summertime, roses and honeysuckle round the door and thatch on the roof – but the artists who drew these cottages for the Christmas calendars did not see the dripping leaks and the rat infested walls, the weeds and the litter in the cold winter months. There was one of these isolated cottages which has now been demolished, and which I had to visit on my first Christmas Day. Old Dr Tench had died on the night before, so a kind friend asked me to share his Christmas lunch with his growing family: and it was from that cheerful atmosphere that I went out in the cold snowy afternoon as dusk came on. It was a long low thatched cottage with a brick path round it, and when I knocked on the door a little girl of about eight

Winter at High Easter *c.* 1906. Dr Tench is in his motor car outside
his surgery

came and let me in. Her entire clothing was a cut down shirt
of her father's, and I remember her blue little feet on the cold
snow-dusted brick. In the downstairs room there were several
children huddled round the table on which there was the end
of a loaf, a jam pot and a pot of tea. I was taken upstairs to the
tiny bedroom, where the mother lay in bed with her latest
child of a week old, she told me she was suffering from 'milk
fever'; by her side was her husband desperately ill with
pneumonia, and there was a small fire in the grate from which
the children had been sent downstairs when I came up.

As I was going out I asked the little girl what she had had
to eat that day, and she said: 'Oh, just bread and jam.'

It is nice to think that that family not only survived, but
the girls were attractive, married well and made good wives,
and gave their elderly parents an extremely comfortable old
age.

I have another memory of that first Christmas in 1930 in the small country community I have described, where much real poverty existed. Charity is a word that is not liked nowadays, but most of what I saw was spontaneous and Christian. Many of the well-to-do regarded it as a duty to old servants or tenants or neighbours, especially at Christmas time, when it was the custom to take round Christmas parcels. These were made up carefully to match the wants of the families: food, clothing, sweets and even small toys.

Dr Tench was dying, but he had nurses in the house. The domestic work of the house was all done by servants, so that Mrs Tench and her sisters would spend long days making up these parcels for the doctor's poor patients who were either on the Parish, or in his dispensary. If they were reasonably near, the parcels would be strapped precariously on the carriers of their bicycles and they would wheel them out, stop for a chat and bicycle home.

But most of the poorer patients were in the villages round: old worn out labourers, widows, or large families on pitifully low wages or with a sick wage earner 'on the club'. These were my job, and my car was loaded up according to the routine round of the day. Mondays and Thursdays were out at High Easter where I ate a picnic lunch in the surgery, returning through the Roothings. Tuesdays and Fridays were out to Takeley, and sometimes Hatfield Broad Oak, with Felsted in the afternoons and sometimes Broxted and Thaxted as well.

A few of the parcels were enormously heavy and included a single huge lump of coal. The best coal was delivered in really large pieces, and it was the job of the gardener's boy to break these up to a reasonable size: but around Christmas time Mrs Tench would go down to the cellar with sticky labels and put the names of families on appropriate lumps, which were brought up and delivered by me. I grumbled at first but was ashamed when I saw the genuine gratitude in the cottages.

Old Bob

TIM WARD

Tim Ward was born at Ilford, but when he was six months old, he and his family went to live at Great Bentley. For forty years he lived in and around Colchester, working on farms and managing a smallholding at Foxash, Ardleigh. He moved to Herefordshire in 1972 and is now a postcard dealer at Ross-on-Wye; he has compiled three books of old postcards.

It was 1942 and new routines had developed in the old farmhouse where we lived, in a part of the Tendring Hundred which had been declared a restricted area, although the wartime restrictions didn't seem to affect us too much. Early in the war my brothers and sister had been sent to Kidderminster when their school had been evacuated. I can still remember their waving as the train full of schoolchildren steamed through Great Bentley Station.

We had a whippet-terrier called Bob and I loved him dearly. When the other children had gone, Bob attached himself to some soldiers at a searchlight unit in the next village a couple of miles away. We heard he was all right but we never saw him.

Meanwhile we had about twenty soldiers billeted with us. Mother cooked for them so we weren't short of food. For a six-year-old lad these were exciting times. Bob's mother had another litter and Dad bought one of them for me; he cost a packet of Players {cigarettes} and a pint of beer. We called him Tim and he grew to the same size as Bob but was a darker shade of ginger.

Saffron Walden County High School orchestra in the Market
Square, Christmas 1960

Christmas was almost with us. Everyone was excited as the children would be coming home for the first time after an absence of two years. My Aunt and Uncle had come from the East End from where they'd been bombed-out. The soldiers were going on leave. I helped Mother put up the decorations which were carefully saved from year to year and stored in a cardboard box under the stairs. The old paper chains, streamer bells and baubles were hung in the same places every year. We dug up last year's Christmas tree (they had roots in those days) and took it inside. Today there's a forty foot fir tree in that garden which was a Christmas tree in 1936. In those days we grew a lot of our food in the garden and kept chickens and geese; and goats to provide milk and cheese.

The Christmas goose hung in the pantry on Christmas Eve

and my brothers and sister were due home that afternoon. My Father, Uncle and I dug parsnips and carrots and picked sprouts for dinner next day. Just as we finished, as if by magic, old Bob appeared and ran around the garden with Tim at his side. At the same time my brothers and sister came walking down the drive. Surprise, astonishment! Coincidence, miracle? Extra-sensory perception, thought transference? We couldn't believe our eyes. Why did Bob return on this particular day? How could he have known that all the family would be at home again? Joy and amazement overwhelmed us, Christmas passed in a haze of happiness. This wartime Christmas sticks in my mind; when my brothers and sister came home and old Bob came too.

The Boar's Head

HONE'S EVERYDAY BOOK

On Christmas-day the following custom has been observed at Hornchurch, in Essex, from time immemorial. The lessee of the tithes, which belong to New College, Oxford, supplies a boar's head dressed and garnished with bayleaves, etc. In the afternoon it is carried in procession into the Mill Field, adjoining the church-yard, where it is wrestled for; and it is afterwards feasted upon at one of the public houses by the

rustic conqueror and his friends, with all merriment peculiar to the season. And here it may be observed that there is another custom at this place, of having a model of an ox's head, with horns, affixed on the top of the eastern end of the chancel of the church. A few years ago it had been suffered to fall into decay, but in the year 1824 it was renewed by the present vicar. This church formerly belonged to the convent on Mount St Bernard in Savoy and it has been suggested that the ox's head, with the horns, may perhaps be the arms or crest of the convent and that the custom, as well as the name of the place, originated from the circumstance. I shall be happy to be informed whether this suggestion be founded on matter of fact; and if not, to what other cause the custom can be assigned.

Edward Thomas's Last Christmas

HELEN THOMAS

Edward Thomas, reviewer and author of many books, only began seriously to write poetry in 1914. In July 1915, he enlisted in the Artists Rifles and in that year was stationed at High Beech near Loughton. The following year he installed his wife and children in a cottage at High Beech. By December

1916 he was stationed at Lydd in Kent, and he expected to be sent to France very soon, but there was no certainty of leave at Christmas. He wrote to Helen, his wife, to say, 'I can't get home for Christmas'. (In her book As It Was *and from which the following extract is taken, she calls Edward 'David'.)*

However, she thought she must prepare for Christmas and busied herself with cakes and puddings and what she could afford of Christmas fare. The children began to make presents for their father and to pack a box for him which included crackers and sweets. The weather was severe; they were poor and their house was dreary, and an indefinable shadow was over them upon that December in 1916.

But a miracle happened. Suddenly this Christmas of all Christmases became the most joyous; the snow-bound forest sparkled like Aladdin's Cave; the house was transformed into a festive bower of holly and ivy and fir boughs, and our listlessness was changed into animated happiness and excitement.

David after all WAS coming home for Christmas!

The letter telling me this arrived by the first post along with one in a strange hand which I opened first, little suspecting what news David's contained. Inside this letter was a cheque for £20 made out to me and signed by the name of a writer of distinction whom I did not know. I stared and stared, and fumbling for the envelope for some explanation found a note from Margaret telling me that she had been asked to forward this to me as a gift from a private fund. What could I not do with £20! I had never had so much in my life. But oh, if only David had been coming home!

Seeing his letter, which in my bewilderment I had forgotten, I read only the first words: 'My dearest, my draft leave will include Christmas after all'. I raced upstairs to the sleeping children. 'Wake up, wake up! Daddy is coming home

for Christmas. He's coming home. He'll be here tomorrow, and I've got £20 to spend, and we'll all have the most wonderful presents; and oh, he's coming home.' Half-crying and half-laughing I lifted the children out of bed, and we danced in a ring and sang 'He's coming home for Christmas' to the tune of 'For he's a jolly good fellow'.

A thick mist hung everywhere when the time came for Edward Thomas to leave his wife and children. His wife stood at the gate and watched him go. He turned and waved, then he was lost in the mist. She heard him call 'coo-ee' until his voice became fainter and fainter. At last there was nothing but the mist and the snow – and silence. Edward Thomas was killed at the Battle of Arras in April 1917.

Poem

EDWARD THOMAS

The following verse was written at High Beech on Christmas Eve 1916.

Out in the dark over the snow
The fallow fawns invisible go
With the fallow doe;
And the winds blow
Fast as the stars are slow.

117

Stealthily the dark haunts round
And, when a lamp goes, without sound
At a swifter bound
Than the swiftest hound,
Arrives, and all else is drowned.

And I and star and wind and deer
Are in the dark together, – near,
Yet far, – and fear
Drums on my ear
In that sage company drear.

How week and little is the light,
All the universe of sight,
Love and delight,
Before the might,
If you have it not, of night.

A Pot of Good Ale

NAT SCRUBY

The poor man will praise it, so hath he good cause,
That all the year eats neither partridge or quaile,
But sets up his rest, and makes up his feast
With a crust of brown bread and a pot of good ale.

And the good old clerk, whose sight waxeth dark,
And ever he thinks the print is too small,
He will see every letter, and say service better,
If he glaze but his eyes with a pot of good ale.

The poet divine that cannot reach wine,
Because that his money does many times fail,
Will hit on the vein to make a good strain,
If he be but inspired with a pot of good ale.

Sunyindale,
Coggleshall
Rhymsteere, 1660

Vignettes

DAVID SMITH

These short pieces are from two books by an Essex farmer. The first is from The Same Sky Over All, *and the others from* No Rain in Those Clouds.

That first Christmas there was a family gathering at Hill House, and the house was blessed by a local parson, the late Reverend Morgan from Great Waltham. As the family rose from their knees after the few short prayers I startled the

gathering by suddenly suggesting: 'Now let's all have some beer!' Even at eight years old I certainly seem to have had the right ideas.

The children usually had their couple of treats every year. Traditionally one was held in the village school at Christmas, and the other on the Rectory lawn at hay-time. The first was notable for the usual decorations (especially long rows of many coloured egg-shells), the distribution of an orange and a bag of sweets to every child, and the piece de resistance, magnificently rowdy musical chairs. The real core of all treats, however, is the tea, and there is a story which my mother's father, the Reverend Walter Wace, told of a small boy at one Christmas treat. He was almost the last survivor, and was fighting a draw with a large sticky doughnut. Grandfather noticed he looked a bit green, and asked him solicitously how he felt.

'Not very well, Sir,' was the reply, 'But I'll have to feel a good deal wuss afore I gives in.'

For many years, through the kindness of some long dead benefactor, large families and old people could obtain parish bread from the church all through the winter, and this was occasionally supplemented by a hundredweight of coal. At East Hanningfield the children's treats were supplemented every January by a mothers' and fathers' treat. The parents were entertained to tea and a concert, and each man on leaving was given a pipe and half an ounce of baccy.

When Father first applied to Sam Tyler for permission to learn to plough, Sam, in company with his brother horsemen said:

'You bring us some beer, and we'll larn you to plough!'

St Mary's church, Saffron Walden, January/February 1947. The
church is two hundred feet long and one of the largest parish
churches in Essex. This view is now completely obscured by houses

Father dutifully obtained and brought the beer, and took
turns driving the various teams up and down the field. When,
after a week or so, his furrows were becoming less devious and
conforming more to the regulation 'straight and narrow', the
teamsman would sit at the top of the field happily drinking
father's 'bribe', and critically watching his pupil. The only
fault the horseman had to find with father was that he picked
it up too quickly!

I was talking to an old cottage woman not long ago, and
what she said is, I think, the best epitaph on what I have tried
to describe as 'The Village Scene'.

'We were all so happy then,' she said.

For many years the whole family had a grand reunion at Link House on Boxing Day. Of his sisters Kate and Lil had married farmers, Sophie a threshing-machine proprietor, who also farmed, and Annie a timber importer. Alice was at home, and married later, after this happy custom had died out. The yard would be filled with the different family equipages. The men would all go rabbiting, the party consisting of perhaps father and his two brothers, Frank and Ted, and such of the five brothers-in-law as happened to be present. The bag on some Boxing Days amounted to as many as one hundred and twenty rabbits, and there is no record of anybody being shot by anyone else, which says a lot for the steadiness of the party.

'A Saturday's moon and a Sunday's full' is what father looks for every Christmas when the firms with which he deals send him either calendars or farming diaries. As soon as the first diary arrives a day or two before Christmas father sits down to it, and hunts for this portent, which, being translated, means a new moon falling on a Saturday and coming to the full on a Sunday. If he finds it, he shakes his head, and the month it falls in is marked off as being bound to bring foul weather, for the full couplet runs as follows:

> A Saturday's moon and a Sunday's full
> Never did no good and never 'ull.

Festive Season

S.L. BENSUSAN

This story was published in Country Fair, *a monthly magazine which folded some years ago. S.L. Bensusan always called these contributions 'papers'. Several volumes of his collected stories have been published and with luck can be found in second-hand bookshops.*

'He married on to me aunt,' Mrs Dunt explained, giving the list of guests to her niece who renders first aid on the great occasion, 'an' he bin a widow man these ten years, pore ole chap. So as we got a empty place, bein' Bill Patient's laid aside, Fred give Adam the invite.'

'He says odd things whiles,' replied the niece. 'Last time we had him up to ours, he talked reglar owd-fashioned. Sez the boys don't work nowadays same as their fathers used to. We all know he wore a good man afore he was tore out, but you don't wanter crake in this world.'

'He'll enjoy hisself for once,' declared Mrs Dunt, the plump kind-hearted wife of Mr Dunt, ex-looker of Waygates, 'an' he'll be friendly.'

Since he retired from work with hard-won savings and a pension, Mr Dunt has given an annual December dinner to half a dozen old friends. By the removal of all surplus furniture and the combination of two tables it is possible for Mr and Mrs Dunt to entertain six guests. Their boys are 'out furrin' as we say, serving the flag.

All went merry as a marriage bell. There was a large joint of beef with potatoes baked round it, there was a pudding to which eight plates could present no problem, there were mince pies and cheese and tobacco and there was beer; there were appetites that could rise to the height of any function.

Mr and Mrs Dunt must save for the great day but it has established their prestige and this year fortune had smiled. Not only had the soldier and sailor sent a contribution, but Mr Dunt had had a wonderful day with the dogs at Market Waldron, returning with four treasury notes of the better kind. Mr Blades the butcher had taken a great part of them for the joint of beef which, if he spoke correctly, was beyond price, and the balance paid for two jars, a dozen bottles of beer and some tobacco. It followed that when the six guests assembled Mr and Mrs Dunt were filled with the proper pride of those who make social history and help deserving friends.

Fancy dress, the Towers Hotel, Clacton, Christmas 1924

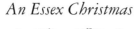

Conversation became general, all spoke at once, all save old Adam Appleflower whose tongue demanded two glasses of beer before it could find expression.

It may be doubted if he would have intruded upon the conversation even then, had not Mr Nix, expert ploughman, launched a spirited attack upon the government, the wages board and farmers who exploit honest men.

'Six poun' a week,' he cried bitterly, as he filled his glass. 'What's that? Now I ast ye. How many days we got in the week? Is it six or sivin?'

'I mind the time,' said Adam, 'when I done me ten hour day f'r ten shillin's a week, an' if so be that rined, I dedn't git nawthen.'

'You should ha' stood up f'r y'rself, Adam,' cried Mr Nix scornfully, 'an' not let folk treed on ye. Everybody gotter stand up f'r hisself in this world.'

'I've know'd plenty o' good men what took ten shillin's come Friday night,' persisted Adam, 'an' glad to git it.'

'More shame f'r 'em,' replied Mr Nix. 'I count ye couldn't ha' had enough to eat.'

'We dedn't,' the veteran admitted. 'Bread and pertaters an' heavy swimmers an' a mossel o' cheese an' a glass o' beer come Saturday night. I've seen me fill me pocket out o' th' meal bin,' he went on as one who is on no terms with shame, 'an' I've bin to th' hedges f'r eggs what th' ducks bin an' laid away. I never set down to sech a spread as this here, except it was time we had our hocky (harvest supper) arter the last waggon come into th' yard, an' that were jest once a year. Th' on'y meat we saw other times was in th' butcher's shop, or when we bin an' fatted a pig.'

'We allus had a hocky at Waygates, too,' remarked Mr Dunt happily, 'beef and rabbit pie an' cheese an' beer an' a singsong.'

'They were days, an' they was songs,' admitted Adam. 'I

liked meself no end. But they've gone. Who sings "The Man in the Moon" nowadays?'

'I mind it,' declared Mr Dunt.

'An' I ain't forgot it,' added Mr Nix.

'Let's sing it, mates,' suggested Mr Dunt cheerfully.

From the overcrowded kitchen, rough untrained voices sang

> Tomorrow I'll borrer
> A great owd balloon
> An' sail right up on high
> An' I'll traipse about till th' stars are out
> An' th' moon come into th' sky

(*chorus*)Th' moon come into th' sky, me boys.
> Th' moon come into th' sky.
> When th' man in th' moon he see me balloon,
> He'll say 'Wha's brought you here?'
> You'll ha' come a long way an' that bin a hot day,
> Step in an' have some beer, me boys,
> Step in an' have some beer.
>   (*chorus*)

The chorus was followed by a moment's silence. Mr Nix broke it.

'We ain't no call to goo far as th' moon,' he remarked, 'bein' we got our beer on th' table.' Here he expressed the sentiments of all the guests.

With beer and tobacco Mr and Mrs Dunt's annual tribute to old friends moved to its happy end.

from

In Memoriam

ALFRED TENNYSON

Tennyson lived at High Beech, a village in Epping Forest, from 1837 to 1840, 'wandering weirdly up and down the house in the small hours, murmuring poetry to himself'. It was to the bells of Waltham Abbey that he addressed the lines 'Ring out the old, ring in the new' in the second of these two extracts. From 1859 to 1871, Anthony Trollope lived at Waltham House (demolished 1936) which Anne Thackeray described as

An Essex Christmas

'a sweet old prim chill house wrapped in snow' in winter.
Trollope described it as 'a rickety old place' and it was here he
wrote The Last Chronicles of Barset.

The time draws near the birth of Christ;
　The moon is hid, the night is still;
　A single church below the hill
Is pealing, folded in the mist.

A single peal of bells below,
　That wakens at this hour of rest
　A single murmur in the breast,
That these are not the bells I know.

Like strangers' voices here they sound,
　In lands where not a memory strays,
　Nor landmark breathes of other days,
But all is now unhallow'd ground.

Ring out wild bells to the wild sky,
　The flying cloud, the frosty light:
　The year is dying in the night;
Ring out wild bells, and let him die.

Ring out the old, ring in the new,
　Ring, happy bells, across the snow:
　The year is going, let him go;
Ring out the false, ring in the true.

Ring out the grief that saps the mind,
　For those that here we see no more;
　Ring out the feud of rich and poor,
Ring in redress to all mankind.

Borley Rectory

HARRY PRICE

*Borley Rectory had the reputation of being the most haunted
house in England. It was built in 1863 by the incumbent, the
Reverend H.D.E. Bull, on the site of a previous rectory.
Apparently the Revd Mr Bull, his family and servants and all
the subsequent inhabitants of the rectory were aware of the
'strange happenings' that occurred there. These 'happenings'
included a ghostly nun, the appearance of a coach and horses,
the ringing of bells, doors mysteriously locked and unlocked,
articles appearing and disappearing, bottles materializing and
hurling about. In 1929 Borley Rectory attracted the attention
of Harry Price, a well-known psychical researcher who became
tenant of the house from May 1937 to May 1938, and wrote
extensively about his investigations. The house was destroyed by
fire soon after Christmas 1938 but the haunting continued.
Contrary to popular supposition, Mr Price said he did not
think that ghosts were more active at Christmas than at other
times of the year. During the latter part of December 1937,
observers reported that practically nothing occurred at Borley
but that the phenomena started early in the New Year. On an
afternoon in early January 1938, Harry Price and a friend
from Oxford settled down after tea in an old study (the Base
Room) at the rectory to await darkness – and what darkness
may bring. . . .*

Just about five o'clock, when it was quite dark in the Base
Room, my friend lit the oil lamp in order that he could

continue his reading. He was sitting near the door, and I was still reclining on the camp-bed. He had hardly picked up his newspaper again, when we were startled by the sound of three short, sharp raps, repeated three times, which appeared to come from the Base Room door, which was in full view of, and quite near, my friend. The Oxford boy was a tyro at ghost-hunting and it rather unnerved him for a moment. *He* could see there was nothing at or near the door. I sat up on the bed.

We waited a minute or so for a repetition of the raps. As these were not forthcoming, I jumped off the bed with the intention of exploring the passage leading to the Base Room. I had hardly crossed the room when both of us heard loud footsteps traversing the passage outside the room. They appeared to be passing our door. Before we had recovered from our surprise – if I can use so mild a term – a door slammed in the back part of the house, near the kitchen quarters.

We rushed out of the Base Room and down the long passage which led to the kitchen, but found nothing disturbed. We had carefully noted the position of each door, and none had been moved by so much as a hairbreadth. All our seals were intact and no one could have entered or left the house without our knowledge. At least, no tangible being could have done so. With our torches we then searched the whole house from attics to cellars without finding anything that would account for the almost incredible noises – incredible under the circumstances – which we had heard. There is a French proverb to the effect that a ghost was never seen by two pairs of eyes; but two pairs of ears undoubtedly heard the raps on the door and the footsteps. And there was nothing ambiguous about the slamming of that door!

A Wildfowler's Diary

SYDNEY TIFFIN

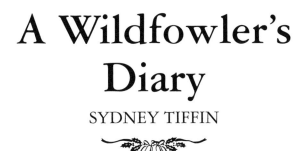

Sydney Tiffin lived at Tillingham and earned his living on the Essex marshes as eel-catcher, winkle-picker and wildfowler; he was the finder of a dead body which was thought to be Stanley Setty, a criminal who, among other things, dealt in second-hand motor cars and forged petrol coupons. An associate claimed to have murdered Setty and dropped his body from an aeroplane into the North Sea. This extract is dated January 1950.

Monday Well I'm up 6.30 this morning because high tide's 8 o'clock. You should see it. The sea sweeps in over the saltings – up to 2 miles some places. One minute there's just mudflats with the widgeon and gulls squeaking overhead. Fifteen minutes later the sea is everywhere, with only patches of bentles (rushes) grass, and sea lavender sticking up.

It was dark and cold when I got up, but by the time I'd waded three miles across the flats to my mother's cottage on the sea-wall the sun was shining through a little old rip in the clouds.

I floated the punt, a 17-footer, and loaded up the punt gun. It takes a pound of shot at a time, and costs about 5s. to fire. The powder is 19s. 6d. a pound, the shot £2 a 28-pound bag, and I have to take a train 30 miles to Colchester to get it. In the war I loaded with any pieces of rubbish I could get, and used bits of old felt hat for wadding.

Wearing a lightish-coloured mac (the birds can spot anything dark on the marshes) I crawl into the boat. Am a bit careful doing this because a punt soon turns over. It's only 3 ft 10 ins wide, draws an inch of water and has to take my weight and the gun, which weighs a hundredweight on its own.

I creep along between the channels made by the bentles, watching for the birds which come in with the tide to eat the zostera grass which only grows in salty places.

Three hours go by. The tide's on the turn and I haven't had a shot. Feel cold, and eyes strained with looking. Then I drift round a bend slap on to a flock of teal about 90 feet away. Move forward in the boat to aim the gun down, because teal

Pier and frozen sea at Southend, 16 January 1905

set low in the water. Fit a cap on the nipple and pull the trigger. But that old cap's got damp. While it hangs fire it makes a hissing sound and the birds hear. They're 6 foot off the water by the time the gun shoots and I don't get one. The punt goes forward with the explosion then comes backward with the recoil. A thick rope from the breech to the seat keeps it from knocking my head off.

I have to go ashore to reload. On the way a flock of black geese rise beside me on the other side of some bentles. Knock two down with the shoulder gun and paddle back to the cottage. I'll get 7d. for the geese.

Tuesday The grey geese are flying inland this morning. Down here we call them 'Gabriel's Hounds', they omen bad weather and storms on the sea. Smells like rain all right, so I won't go punt-gunning today.

Walk along the sea-wall looking for anything that might be washed up, and remember the war when my job was to put a rope around any floating mines and beach them. That was a bad old job. The sea's been my living since I was eight and helped coil ropes on my dad's fishing smack. At 14 I was sailing her (a 20-tonner) the 30 miles between Burnham and Clacton, and at 21 they were asking me to be master on a smack out of Grimsby. And I'd never seen the inside of a school.

Along the saltings with the sea lap-lapping away I think how things have changed since I was a little old tot. Them days there was 17 or 18-punt gunners in these parts, and there used to be dozens of people winkle-picking and eel-prytching along the shore. But kids haven't the patience now. You don't see any winkle-pickers, there's only the coastguard and me wild-fowling and nobody makes punt guns any more. Mine's been in the family 30 years, and bought secondhand at that.

The Square, Tillingham. St Nicholas Church, the Cock Inn and
Village Pump

It's raining. I wade back to Tillingham, change out of my
sea-boots and go round to The Cap and Feathers for a game of
darts with Fred.

In the evening before dusk starts closing in I go back to the
sea-wall and bait a couple of hundred lines which I leave
overnight. Then I go to the Parish Hall for the whist drive.
Won a bottle of sherry last week.

Wednesday Hauled in the night lines this morning and
unhooked about 40 fish, some weighing up to 2 pounds. Took
them round and sold them straight off. Fish and wild duck
are easy to sell but the geese are hard to get rid of round here.
People get tired of them, I guess.

Walked round to Mr Attenborough's decoy pond. It's about
the last left in these parts. The wild duck see the decoys and

settle down on the lake. Then dogs run round the edge making the ducks swim to the V shaped end, where a net catches them.

Had a letter from the Catchment Board offering me a job filling in the dykes. Am glad of it because the wild-fowling season ends on February 17, and that's mostly my living. Until it opens again on August 12, I pick up what I can.

This is really my day off. The travelling cinema comes to the Parish Hall, and I always go. Call at Mrs Hubbard's sweet-shop for the rest of my sweets first.

After the pictures, go round The Cap and Feathers for a game of darts with Fred.

Thursday The day breaks fine. The sea lies over the marshes as smooth and quiet as a sheet of ice. I creep along in the punt watching the sky for a flock of birds to settle. The sun is still down and the light is a sort of misty grey. Just right for punt-gunning – you get it at early dawn, in the evening before the dusk grows, and on a moonlight night.

I am over the Dengie flats where I happed on the murdered body when I see a cloud of black geese settling down out of the sky. I paddle toward the spot, very slow, just really helping the boat to drift. There must be no noise.

The bentles open out and I see the birds ahead about 200 yards. The gun will kill up to half a mile, but for a proper shot you need to be within 90 yards. At about a 100 yards I ease back a bit to bring the gun muzzle up. I pull the trigger, and after the explosion a cloud of black smoke hangs in front of me so I can't see what's happened.

Then I'm up with the shoulder gun firing on the birds that are wounded or stunned. It's practically the little gun that gets the most if you understand it.

When I've picked them all up I've got 40 geese. A good bag. The most I ever got with one shot was 60, but I did know a man as got 100 with one shot.

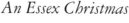

I take the geese back to the cottage, re-load and paddle out again. The light is really too bright but I'm lucky. I steal up on a flock of duck and get 11. I'll get nine bob a pair for the duck.

Friday Hear I've got to go up to London about Mr Setty next week. I don't like that. There's too many people in London.

I got a £1,000 for finding the body, but it's been a lot of trouble. They didn't want to pay me the reward because the head was missing and I had to get solicitors to help me. And here's another thing. I've found nine bodies one time and another on the marshes, and I've always got five bob from the police. But I didn't get the five bob this time. Why?

One thing, I wish my wife was alive to share the reward. The most we ever saved together was £50. We used to live in a cottage on the sea-wall, and she had to walk 4 miles to Tillingham for the shopping. One day, seven years ago she dropped dead 50 yards from our door. I reckon if I'd had that money then she'd be alive today.

White January

C. HENRY WARREN

The scene is Finchingfield in January 1940; the account of a snowbound community is from England is a Village.

For days we have been almost cut off from the outside world – a community of some nine hundred souls huddled together in a white waste of snow. 'Snowy Tuesday', some of the old folk say, recalling with peasant exactitude a bitter fall in 1881. Others call it 'Black Tuesday'. Snowy or black, however, we of a younger generation have hitherto been a little inclined to doubt their tales of outlying farms and cottages that were isolated for a week on end and of snow that drifted so high it was possible to walk over the tops of the hedges. Such things do not happen, here in the kindly south. So we said, and credited their tales to the proneness of old people for exaggerating the happenings of years gone by. Let them boast, it does no harm, anyway!

But now the same thing has happened in our own time. There *are* farms and cottages in the 'uplands' (as we say, though nowhere hereabouts is more than three hundred feet above sea-level) that neither the baker nor the grocer nor even the postman can get near; and all around the village there *are* drifts of snow in the sunken lanes so high you can walk over the tops of the hedges. Thus humbled, we shall perhaps listen a little less incredulously in the future to the tales of our elders. And no doubt we, in our turn, shall seem as prone to the exaggerations of old age when we tell of the snows of this white January.

It is one of the merits of village life, as well as one of the penalties, that we are, even in the most propitious days, so closely interdependent one on another. And when such inclement weather as this shuts us away from the world, we are even more closely united. If there was kindness among us before, it is more than trebled now. If there was envy, hatred or malice, it seems for the moment to have been forgotten. Perhaps there is an element of fear compelling us to this unstinted kindness, a faint echo in us from the days when, to an extent not even the severest hardships can inspire to-day,

men and women were forced to find safety in communal endeavour. Or perhaps it is nothing more than excitement, engendered by a spectacle in which, whether we will or no, we are all compelled to play our part. The same dead sky hangs over us all, day after day. The same snow comes flaking down on the just and the unjust alike. And the same uncanny silence fills us all, even to the most unsusceptible among us, with premonitions of we know not what.

Before the snow came, we used to be wakened in the morning by the sound of men going off to work. Voices below the Causeway told us that Tom Crutchly and Arthur Small were passing one another on their bicycles as they pedalled out of the village in the early dusk. 'Nice mornin', Tom!' 'Aye, it is that.' And then silence again, broken only by the sound of the stream purling by the roadside. But once Tom and Arthur had gone by, punctual as the sun itself, others would soon follow.

The Parade, Burnham-on-Crouch, 1958

It was amusing to lie abed, pleasantly half-awake, picking out the passers-by by mere weight and rhythm of their tread. Easiest of all to recognize, of course, was Sam Merriman's, the blacksmith. At any time Sam shuffles rather than walks; but when he goes across to his forge, first thing in the morning, his heavy boots are still unlaced and then his usual shuffle would sound even sprightly by comparison. Kettle in hand, he ambles down the road to the forge, to boil some water for the morning cup of tea; and it is with this first unbuttoned appearance of Sam that the day really begins. His loud voice and his louder laughter, as he greets whoever comes along, are the cock-crow announcing the dawn, and any sounds and voices, earlier than his, are mere shy, hesitant bird-calls, timorously awaiting the master-herald of all. Sam has a word for everybody and everybody has a word for Sam; and those he does not meet in the road itself, he calls up to in their bedrooms: nobody is allowed to sleep on once Sam has appeared on the scene.

But now it is all quite different. No Tom or Arthur goes pedalling past, called from bed each morning for a pittance on some far-off farm. And when Sam does appear, the day is already so far advanced that nobody could rely on such a belated cock-crow. In that cold silence when the snow throws its first white light on to the ceiling, it is almost as if the end of the world had happened overnight, and, unaccountably, we were the only souls left alive in a blank and muffled world. At last, however, there are voices – voices unnaturally clear, and as it were suspended, because unaccompanied by the sound of passing feet, in a vacuum. And then, once we are up, we see what all the mystery is about. There is nothing the snow has not clung to and changed past all knowing. Roof and tree, road and garden, all have been fashioned anew in the night by a hand of miraculous cunning and to the whim of a mind that loves not colour.

And down by Mark Thurston's cottage, under the knot of elms we had thought so friendly and so familiar, half a dozen men have suddenly appeared from nowhere with a couple of horses and the village snow-plough. Monkish in their sacks, which they wear over their heads, the two corners tucked one into the other, the men handle the cumbersome implement that has lain on the grass by the roadside all the year, its massive shares decorated with cowslips in spring and hidden under a foam of kexes in summer. While some of them attend to the harnessing of the horses, others stand by, flinging their arms about like flails, in an attempt to stir some sort of warmth in their shivering bodies.

Whereupon, of course, Mark appears at his door, with not even a jacket to shield his seventy-seven years, and, what really is unusual, without his cap. No old farm-hand ever dreams of going about with his head uncovered, any more than he would dream of picking a bunch of wild flowers ('*them* ol' things: now if they was taters, I'd understand'), and so there is always a suggestion of nakedness in the sight of a hatless villager, his pale, unsunned brow contrasting so vividly with the remainder of his ruddy, weathered face. In Mark the oddness is emphasized this morning by the reflection of the snow on his high, shining forehead. With both hands thrust deep in his pockets, he watches the men struggling with their plough.

'Bless us, Bob,' he says, 'it's a rummy sort of furrer you'll draw this morning. And hadn't you better stick a twig o' something in Gipsy's forelock to keep them ol' flies away?'

But nobody takes any notice. Mark's little jokes are not always as keenly appreciated as he thinks they are; and anyway, the men are too cold this morning to pay attention to him. 'Now then, Gipsy! Come up, Dimint!' And the hooded men follow their cumbersome plough up the road, cleaving a wide furrow through the snow that curls over and breaks, like

Near Finchingfield, 31 December 1927

the ploughed stubble in autumn. Mark turns away, shutting his door behind him.

For awhile yet the village maintains its empty silence. Double-thatched now, with straw and snow, the cottage roofs project their picturesque angles against the deadened sky. Over Goose End the ruined windmill flaunts its broken sails, set at Miller's Pride till they fall and ill able to support the weight of snow lodged on their upper edges. Gardens there are none, and every bush is a frozen fountain. Our meagre river, running through the centre of the village, is indistinguishable now from the Green that rims its banks. At other times, it alternates swiftly from a convenient mirror (beloved of photographers) for the reflection of the surrounding cottages to a muddy stench that causes the passers-by to pinch their noses in disgust; but to-day both mirror and stench are sealed in ice.

Buried somewhere beneath its white, unruffled surface are the inviting slides that traverse it from end to end – slides where the children of the village have enjoyed themselves as never since they were born and where even the farm-hands, returning from the fields in the early dusk, could not resist the temptation to drop their bicycles against the bridge and take a flying turn or two before they went home to tea. Later on, no doubt, somebody will brush the snow away, or at least enough of it to uncover the precious slides. But it will be beyond their power to restore the simple sport to the pitch of ecstasy it engendered all last week and the best part of the week before. For then there was a moon. And while the frost dropped silver stars on the roofs and spun from every branch and twig a hoary lace that only the morning would discover, lads and girls, and children who should long ago have been abed, sped over the glassy river, wings at their heels, and filled the blacked-out village with their laughing voices.

The Green is the hub of the village and much admired by our visitors. Four roads intersect it, pale ribbons that cut the green grass into unacademic triangles; and the meeting-place of these four roads is a narrow brick bridge adequate enough for the trickle of water which, in summer, flows underneath it, but totally inadequate for the amount of traffic which such a convergence of roads must necessarily cause.

However, it is a charming bridge in its simple, unhistoric way, and the number of accidents its inadequacy has so far occasioned is not yet sufficiently impressive to stir our Parish Council to do anything about it. Not that we have ever urged the Council to do anything about it. On the whole, we are a conservative people and (often quite justifiably) suspicious of innovations. Besides, from time immemorial the bridge has been the haunt of such old men as Mark, who, turned out of the pub before their argument has reached a satisfactory

conclusion, may surely be allowed to lean somewhere and finish their talk in peace?

But now there is nobody leaning against the bridge. There is nobody anywhere. Then one by one people begin to appear. A door opens, and a woman wrapped up in a shawl tied over her head like a rabbit's ears picks her slow way across the Green; or another door opens, and a man with a broom makes a futile effort to brush back the snow that has heaped over his step, like Canute trying to push back the tide.

The two butchers shops, apparently, do not deem it necessary to open this morning; and the grocer's shop, whatever activities may be going on inside, presents an obstinately inhospitable front. Only the post office is open. For Miss Dickson, though nobody would guess it from her jocular manner and her warm-hearted concern for the welfare of all of us, is a Civil Servant, and the Civil Service allows no concessions, or few, to the whims and eccentricities of country behaviour in general. Snow or no snow, business must go on as usual in the post office – or as nearly usual as the circumstances will allow. For even in the post office punctuality has been nullified by this heaping snow. The mail-van has not yet managed to get through to the village, and the postmen, who dare not do the sensible thing and go home for a hot drink and a second breakfast, must make the best they can of an enforced idleness, kicking their heavy heels on the floor and flinging their arms about, till Miss Dickson's imperilled sweet-bottles rattle on the shelves and even she can hold them in good humour no longer.

Nor is it only the postmen who are a little ruffled in temper by this unaccommodating weather. Tradesmen, tired of running their cars up roads that lead nowhere but to a blank wall of snow, are all inclined to be a little brusque these days. And as the first novelty wears off, even the farm-hands, stolid enough as a rule, are getting weary of being sent so far

afield, spade in hand, to help the unemployed dig away the drifts.

Only in Goose End is there no appreciable sign of petulence. And the cause of such geniality, of course, is Sam Merriman. For Sam all this is welcome holiday: no horses to shoe, no spare parts to mend, nothing to do but exactly what he chooses to do. And what he chooses to do is as nearly nothing as makes no difference. Late to rise, therefore, at last he comes out into the roadway, shuffling along and kicking up the powdery snow like a ten-year-old. Carrying his broom over his shoulder, he volunteers to sweep anybody's snow away for them; and what his endeavours lack in effectuality, they certainly make up for in jocularity.

'Now then, midear: what can I do for you?' And he begins brandishing his broom about, as if the gestures of a magician were what the heaped-up doorstep needs, and not good hard work.

Frost and Snow

HUMPHREY PHELPS

1814   January, average temperature below 27 °F.

1837   20 January, temperature -4 °F. Players wore skates to play cricket on frozen Gosfield Lakes.

1841   January, deep snow at Colchester.

1854   4 January, heavy snowfall, deep snow at Colchester. Railway services between Colchester and Norwich suspended.

1860   Mid-December, skating on Wanstead Pond. Christmas Day temperature 8 °F.

1881   18 January, blizzard lasting twenty-four hours. Houses and trains buried in snow, lifeboats capsized, barges sunk, parts of Southend Pier swept away. Snowdrifts of up to seventeen feet.

1890   13 December, skating on River Can at Chelmsford.

1891   Early January, over two thousand skating on river between Chelmsford and Maldon.

1893   Early January, Ice Carnival on The Cutting.

1894   5 January, temperature at Chelmsford 0 °F.

1895   February, very severe frosts cause great hardships.

1906   White Christmas Day. Roads blocked. Heaviest snowfall for fifteen years at Clacton.

1917   Long cold winter.

1918   January, heavy snow.

1927   White Christmas. Roads blocked. Finchingfield, Bardfield, Dunmow, Halstead isolated for a week.

1928   January, snow.

Skating on the Blackwater at Maldon, 1892

1938   White Christmas. Snow every day in Essex from mid-December.

1939   Snow at end of December.

1940   January, snow, severe frost. Heavy snowstorm for three days middle of month.

1941   Cold winter with snow.

1942   January, snow fell at Romford on seventeen days; and on nineteen days in February.

1945   January, very cold, snow on ground half the month.

1947   20 January, very severe weather started; and continued for two months. Temperatures down to -5 °F. Some rivers frozen. Snowdrifts of fifteen feet.

1950   Coldest December since 1890. Snow at Romford for eighteen days.

1951   1 January, heavy snowfall.

1962   Coldest Christmas since 1897. Snow fell on Boxing Day, most of Essex under snow until March 1963. 1962–3 coldest winter since 1740.

1968   Snow in January. Some rivers frozen.

1969   February, snow on ground at Earls Colne for a fortnight.

1970   White Christmas. Heavy snowfalls on Christmas Day and Boxing Day.

1978   Snow at end of December.

1979   Snow in January.

1980   Snow in December.

1981   Coldest December since 1890, with snow at Colchester for three weeks.

1982   January, snow.

1985   January, temperature fell to -12 °C and snow at Colchester for a fortnight.

Plough Monday

CHRISTOPHER KETTERIDGE

Christopher Kerridge was born during the early years of this century and lived in the Essex village of Ashdon.

Plough Monday is no longer remembered or celebrated in the manner which the old-time farm workers accorded it. Very few today have even heard of it or what it meant to those old labourers of an almost forgotten era in the history of East Anglian farming. Falling on the first Monday after Epiphany, it marked the commencement of the winter ploughing season; when the agricultural workers returned to their toil after a short but unpaid Christmas holiday. Apart from this it was a day on which the out-of-work labourers held their traditional demonstrations.

I recall almost 70 years ago the spectacle of a dozen or more farmworkers hauling a ponderous single-breasted wooden beam plough through the streets of my native village. There was snow on the roads at the time which facilitated their task, for the steel segments of a wagon's tyre fitted to the undersides of the heavy slide on which it was mounted allowed it to slip more easily over the frozen surface. These sturdy plough-slides were very necessary in transporting the plough from field to field for, unlike the all-metal variety, the wooden beam plough had no wheels whatever. I recall so well the din they were creating as they hauled their burden, the symbol of their trade; but I learned in after years this was their usual method of attracting the attention of all and sundry to their desperate need.

In the severe winters of those days, when most of the seasonal tasks had been completed, or maybe the stress of weather rendered them no longer possible, many labourers were thrown out of work. Only the key workers like the 'Hossmen', the 'Stockmen' and the 'Shepherds' would be eenabled to carry on for, whatever the conditions, the farm animals had to be fed and cared for. The casual hands who carried out the hedging and ditching, the threshing and all its allied tasks, together with all the odd jobs about the farm, were turned away. In those days, there was absolutely no help for these unfortunates. They existed as best they could in conditions of severe hardship. It was small wonder they resorted to poaching, for what man worth his salt would stand idly by and watch his wife and family starve, when the fields and woods teemed with rabbits and game?

To these unfortunate men, 'Plough Monday' afforded an opportunity to collect a few shillings from their better off fellow-villagers to alleviate, in a small measure, the suffering of their families. On that important date they would haul around the traditional plough, calling at all the houses in the village where they might reasonably expect a small donation. The Squire's, the Parson's, the Shopkeepers', the Butcher's and the Baker's; the last three of whom often paid in kind. When, as sometimes happened, they encountered an unwilling patron, the threat to draw a furrow across their lawn or front garden in default of a donation was often resorted to. Seldom, if ever, was this high-handed action carried out; for it usually produced the desired result when just a few coppers were sufficient to placate the demonstrators.

Snow Fights

SPIKE MAYS

This is another extract from Reuben's Corner. *Eventually Reuben's Corner and Essex were left behind and Spike Mays was 'Away to Canterbury, the army, and a life that would never be the same again'.*

In the winter months our return journey from school was often in total darkness. There were no street or road lights and the stars would not be out until much later. If there was snow or ice on the roads and fields we would be late home. Not because we were unable to negotiate the roads but because we would make slides, toboggan runs, snowmen, and would have long, fierce snow-fights. In the snow-fighting there were often minor casualties. The big boys, the cunning ones who had seen a winter or two, used to cheat. They would press and press their snowballs until they were almost blocks of ice. Sometimes they would even slip a small stone into a soft snowball. There would be cut cheeks, blood on the snow and other fights – fiercer fights – without snow. Each End would challenge other Ends and Bartlow Hamlet to make the longest and most slippery slide in the road. Some were longer than cricket pitches but it was great fun to see the glowing cheeks, to hear the shrieks of joy and laughter as novices fell on their backsides. And when we had had enough or were getting hungry we would cover the long slides with snow so that no one could see them, hoping to see old men fall on them and curse like mad.

The toboggan runs were made on the steep slope of Hilly

Tobogganing on the Essex/Hertfordshire border

Meadow, behind Cobby Webb's farm, or Chapel Farm, to give it its right title. We made our own toboggans or sledges from boxes scrounged from old Vic Eason, the village shopkeeper – father of Reg, Mabel Eason's husband. If Bill Smith the blacksmith was not too busy making great iron shoes for the Suffolk Punches and Clydesdales, or was not bent in two with his crippling rupture, he would put iron runners on a sledge for sixpence. Then off we would go to Hilly Meadow, sometimes in total darkness to whip down the steep slopes like lightning. A small stream ran along the bottom of Hilly Meadow. On its bank there was a great hawthorn hedge, quite ten feet high. If the sledges were overloaded, or we did not put out our feet quickly enough to do some useful braking, we would tear through the hawthorn hedge and land in the stream. Inevitably there would be casualties here, too, mostly gashed cheeks from the hawthorn spikes, ripped clothing or a total immersion in icy water.

From the Newspapers

HUMPHREY PHELPS

A certain Farmer, near Stratford in Essex, who was possessed of a very large Quantity of Wheat, some of which he has sold at Eighteen and some at Twenty Pounds a Load, at length refused to part with any more under Twenty-two Pounds a Load, but the price falling he was forced to break into his Stacks, and out of Eighty Loads, found near one third of it destroyed by Rats.

The Ipswich Journal
17 December 1757

A scheme is now under consideration for every parish in Great Britain to furnish four recruits for the army, which, it is said will raise about 50,000 men. They are to have a bounty, and to be discharged at the end of three years, as an inducement to their speedy entering.

The Chelmsford Chronicle
19 December 1777

We learn that there are this year three claimants to the ancient endowment of £5 bequeathed for the benefit of 'ye poore debtors' confined in Springfield gaol at Christmas time. The amount received by each will be £5. 13. 4d., which will enable them to 'keep Christmas' even in gaol in right genial style, having previously, however, had to undergo the trifling

drawback of being 'boarded' for a week at the county expense, in order to qualify themselves for the gift.

The Chelmsford Chronicle
27 December 1867

This Act came into operation on Wednesday. The Act prohibits the employment of children under eight years of age in agricultural labour, and also enforces a separation of the sexes in field work. Gang masters and gang mistresses are to be licenced, applications for licences at 1s. each being granted at the discretion of two justices of the peace, with the right to appeal to the Quarter Sessions in case of the refusal of applications. Penalties are prescribed in case of non-compliance with the Act.

The Gloucester Journal
4 January 1868

Last week fifty loads of wood was cut down in Epping Forest by the order of the Earl of Tylney, and distributed to fifty poor widows of the parish of Barking, according to annual custom.

Kentish Gazette
Wednesday 4 January to Saturday 7 January 1769

Last Friday was New Year's Day. But it was also much more than that. It was the day which brought into operation the Liberal Government's Old Age Pensions Act! As a result of the passing of this beneficent and magnificent measure, upwards of half a million aged poor were entitled on Friday to walk into Post Offices and claim as their right a weekly pension ranging from one shilling to five. The granting of this boon to veterans of the industrial battle of life will ever remain a landmark in the history of the Liberal Party. New Year's Day saw the dawning of a new era for the deserving poor. Aged men and women who could not have lived many

more weeks without being overtaken by the dread shadow of the workhouse dragged their feeble frames to the nearest Post Office and drew their State pension, many shedding tears of joy as they received the money. In many country districts the pensioners were entertained at social gatherings by their richer brethren, and messages of gratitude were sent to the Premier and Mr Lloyd George. . . .

At Braintree the Town Band paraded the streets playing 'Hail! Smiling Morn' and other jubilant tunes; at Halstead the day was ushered in with the firing of cannon and closed with a torchlight procession; and at Haverhill there was a tea and entertainment at the Town Hall.

The Bury Free Press
9 January 1909

Near Brightlingsea

There is now at Friday-Hill House, in the parish of Chingford, Essex, the oak table upon which King Charles knighted the loin of beef. The house is now the property of — Heathcote Esq. It is a large building, containing more than 30 rooms, in a dilapidated state, but it is now undergoing considerable repair. Report has it that it was originally a hunting seat of Queen Elizabeth. The table, thick and of a clumsy appearance, is made of English oak, which, from the effect of time, is a little decayed.

The County Chronicle
12 January 1830

Last week Mr Harvey, Supervisor of Excise at Brentwood, received information of a Party of smugglers being on the Road from Billericay towards Brentwood, with several Horse-Loads of Tea and other Smuggled Goods. He immediately applied to one Serjeant Lightfoot of the 34th Regiment of Foot, now on a Recruiting Party and quartered at Brentwood, to assist him in making a Seizure of the same, who, together with three new Recruits, the Supervisor and three other Excise-Officers, armed with Pistols etc., went on Horseback between Twelve and One in the Morning towards Billericay to meet them; and about Three Quarters of a mile beyond the Turnpike leading to Hutton met about 20 horses loaded, and as many Men well armed to attend them. They imprudently, without considering the Inequality of Number, fell on the Smugglers Sword in Hand, but were soon forced to give way, being overpowered; the Supervisor, Serjeant and Recruits behaved with Courage and Resolution, and had the others done the same, there doubtless would have been much Mischief done, if not Murder, on both sides. The Supervisor presented a Pistol at one of the Smugglers, who in a sneering manner bid him put it up as he would certainly come off the Worst if he went to that Work; but before he could make any

Reply was knocked down. The Smugglers proceeded on their journey towards London, went through Brentwood in Triumph about Two, and were seen to go through Ilford about Four. One of the Smugglers received a violent Cut with a Sword on the side of his Head, which almost took off his Cheek; the Serjeant received six Wounds on his Head, one of which it is feared will prove mortal. The Supervisor is dangerously wounded and his recovery is very doubtful; and one of the Recruits is likely to lose his Arm.

The Northampton Mercury
13 January 1772

On Saturday last a bargain was made by Mr Hamilton of Colchester with a miller in the neighbourhood of Ardleigh, seven miles from the town, for 30 quarters of Bran to be carried by a stage coach, with six horses, from the Miller's house to the Stone's End, Colchester, in two hours, which, if Mr Hamilton performed, he was to pay an under price for the bran, and if he carried 40 quarters, he was to have it gratis. So great an improbability was it thought that many considerable wagers were laid; however the 40 quarters (near six ton) were carried 20 minutes within the time, to the astonishment of hundreds of spectators. The load upon the coach made it more than 16 feet high, and several persons rode on it to balance the bulk.

The Newcastle Courant
15 January 1780

Billericay, Essex January 18
The snow here affords the most amazing and melancholy scene ever known by the oldest man living, it being from six to ten feet deep in the roads, which renders them entirely impassable for carriages. The Rochford coach came in here on Saturday, but could get no further, neither that or the Billericay coach attempted to go either way till Wednesday, when both set out

for London; the post boy came in here on Saturday and attempted to go to Rochford, but could not. About thirty men have been employed two days in cutting avenues through the snow in the several roads leading from the town.

The Chester Chronicle
29 January 1776

Coggeshall Ditty

ANON.

The horse and mare live thirty years
Without the aid of wines or beers,
The cow and sheep at 15 die
And nothing know of rum or rye.
The dog at 14 years packs in
And never tastes of Scotch or gin.
The modest, sober, bone-dry hen
Lays eggs for years, and dies at ten.
The cat in milk or water soaks
And then at 12 short years it croaks.
All animals are strictly dry;
They sinless live, and early die
But sinful, ginful, rum soaked men
Live on till three score years and ten.
And some of us, the mighty few,
Stay pickled till we're 92.

Acknowledgements

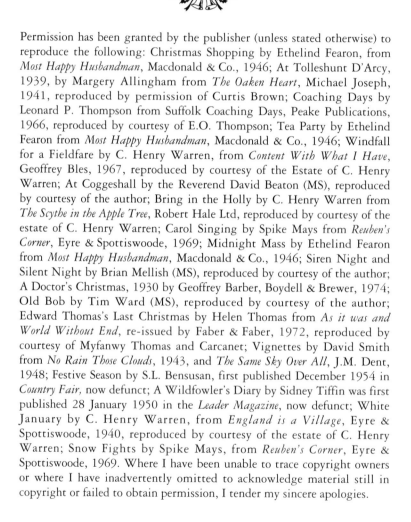

Permission has been granted by the publisher (unless stated otherwise) to reproduce the following: Christmas Shopping by Ethelind Fearon, from *Most Happy Husbandman*, Macdonald & Co., 1946; At Tolleshunt D'Arcy, 1939, by Margery Allingham from *The Oaken Heart*, Michael Joseph, 1941, reproduced by permission of Curtis Brown; Coaching Days by Leonard P. Thompson from Suffolk Coaching Days, Peake Publications, 1966, reproduced by courtesy of E.O. Thompson; Tea Party by Ethelind Fearon from *Most Happy Husbandman*, Macdonald & Co., 1946; Windfall for a Fieldfare by C. Henry Warren, from *Content With What I Have*, Geoffrey Bles, 1967, reproduced by courtesy of the Estate of C. Henry Warren; At Coggeshall by the Reverend David Beaton (MS), reproduced by courtesy of the author; Bring in the Holly by C. Henry Warren from *The Scythe in the Apple Tree*, Robert Hale Ltd, reproduced by courtesy of the estate of C. Henry Warren; Carol Singing by Spike Mays from *Reuben's Corner*, Eyre & Spottiswoode, 1969; Midnight Mass by Ethelind Fearon from *Most Happy Husbandman*, Macdonald & Co., 1946; Siren Night and Silent Night by Brian Mellish (MS), reproduced by courtesy of the author; A Doctor's Christmas, 1930 by Geoffrey Barber, Boydell & Brewer, 1974; Old Bob by Tim Ward (MS), reproduced by courtesy of the author; Edward Thomas's Last Christmas by Helen Thomas from *As it was and World Without End*, re-issued by Faber & Faber, 1972, reproduced by courtesy of Myfanwy Thomas and Carcanet; Vignettes by David Smith from *No Rain Those Clouds*, 1943, and *The Same Sky Over All*, J.M. Dent, 1948; Festive Season by S.L. Bensusan, first published December 1954 in *Country Fair,* now defunct; A Wildfowler's Diary by Sidney Tiffin was first published 28 January 1950 in the *Leader Magazine*, now defunct; White January by C. Henry Warren, from *England is a Village*, Eyre & Spottiswoode, 1940, reproduced by courtesy of the estate of C. Henry Warren; Snow Fights by Spike Mays, from *Reuben's Corner*, Eyre & Spottiswoode, 1969. Where I have been unable to trace copyright owners or where I have inadvertently omitted to acknowledge material still in copyright or failed to obtain permission, I tender my sincere apologies.